Y

AFRICAN RELIGION
WORLD RELIGIONS

by
Aloysius M. Lugira

☑ Facts On File, Inc.

AFRICAN RELIGION
World Religions
Copyright © 1999 by Aloysius M. Lugira

Facts On File, Inc.
11 Penn Plaza
New York, NY 10001

Library of Congress Cataloging-in-Publication Data
Lugira, Aloysius Muzzanganda.
    African religion / by Aloysius M. Lugira.
       p.   cm.—(World Religions)
    Includes bibliographical references and index.
    Summary: Provides a history of African Religion and its basic beliefs, discussing oral tradition, ideas of the Supreme Being, rites and rituals, sacred spaces and places, and mystical forces.
       ISBN 0-8160-3876-7 (alk. paper)
       1. Africa—Religion—Juvenile literature.   [1. Africa—Religion.]
       I. Title.   II. Series.
    BL2400.L84   1999
    299'.6—dc21   99-10254

Facts On File books are available at special discounts when purchased in bulk quantities for businesses, associations, institutions, or sales promotions. Please call our Special Sales Department in New York at (212) 967–8800 or (800) 322–8755.

You can find Facts On File on the World Wide Web at http://www.factsonfile.com.

Developed by Brown Publishing Network, Inc. Series design by Trelawney Goodell. Design production by Carroll Conquest/Brown Publishing Network, Inc. Photo research by Martha Friedman.

Photo credits:
Cover: Mask of the Bakwele people of the Democratic Republic of Congo in Central Africa. Werner Forman/Art Resource, N.Y. Kente design courtesy of Kwasi Sarkodie-Mensah; *Title page:* Mask from the Dan people of Ivory Coast. Courtesy of the Charles and Blanche Derby Collection. Photo by David Stansbury; *Table of Contents page:* Nigerian women perform a Benin dance, using decorated gourds as musical accompaniment. J.H. Morris/Panos Pictures; *Pages 6–7:* www.corbis.com/Dave Hamman, ABPL; *14:* Maryknoll Fathers and Brothers; *15:* Courtesy, Museum of Fine Arts, Boston; *18:* Marcus Rose/Panos Pictures; *20–21:* Jeremy Hartley/Panos Pictures; *24:* J. Corso, M. M./Maryknoll Photo Library; *27:* Kenya Information Office/Maryknoll Photo Library; *31:* The Minneapolis Institute of Arts; *34–35:* John Pemberton III; *39:* The Nelson-Atkins Museum of Art, Kansas City, Missouri (Purchase: Nelson Trust through the generosity of Donald J. and Adele C. Hall, Mr. and Mrs. Herman Robert Sutherland, and anonymous donor, and the exchange of Nelson Gallery Foundation properties); *40:* www.corbis.com/Sharna Balfour, ABPL; *46–47:* Photograph courtesy of the Royal Ontario Museum (950.257.56) © ROM; *50:* Courtesy of the author; *54:* Werner Forman/Art Resource, N.Y.; *57:* Courtesy of the Charles and Blanche Derby Collection. Photo by David Stansbury; *60:* Photograph courtesy of Lakeview Museum of Arts and Sciences, Richard K. Miller Collection, 85.40.5; *62–63:* Eric Miller/Panos Pictures; *66:* C. Barton/ Middle East Pictures; *74:* Courtesy of the author; *77:* The Nelson-Atkins Museum of Art, Kansas City, Missouri (Purchase: Nelson Trust); *80:* Anna Tully/Panos Pictures; *82–83:* John A. Daar; *85:* www.corbis.com/North Carolina Museum of Art; *86:* © National Geographic Society Image Collection/Gilberth Grosvenor; *89:* Courtesy of the Charles and Blanche Derby Collection. Photo by David Stansbury; *92–93:* David Reed/Panos Pictures; *95:* Eric Miller/Panos Pictures; *96:* Maryknoll Picture Library; *99:* Christine Osborne/Middle East Pictures; *100:* Courtesy of the author; *104–105:* Catherine Smith, Impact Visuals; *107:* Corbis/Reuters; *110:* Photograph courtesy of the Royal Ontario Museum (924.9.8) © ROM; *111:* Hirshhorn Museum and Sculpture Garden, Smithsonian Institution, gift of Joseph H. Hirshhorn, 1972. ©1999 Estate of Pablo Picasso/Artists Rights Society (ARS), New York.

Printed in the United States of America
RRD/PKG 10 9 8 7 6 5 4 3 2 1
This book is printed on acid-free paper.

TABLE OF CONTENTS

Preface

The 20th century is sometimes called a "secular age," meaning, in effect, that religion is not an especially important issue for most people. But there is much evidence to suggest that this is not true. In many societies, including the United States, religion and religious values shape the lives of millions of individuals and play a key role in politics and culture as well.

The World Religions series, of which this book is a part, is designed to appeal to both students and general readers. The books offer clear, accessible overviews of the major religious traditions and institutions of our time. Each volume in the series describes where a particular religion is practiced, its origins and history, its central beliefs and important rituals, and its contributions to world civilization. Carefully chosen photographs complement the text, and a glossary and bibliography are included to help readers gain a more complete understanding of the subject at hand.

Religious institutions and spirituality have always played a central role in world history. These books will help clarify what religion is all about and reveal both the similarities and differences in the great spiritual traditions practiced around the world today.

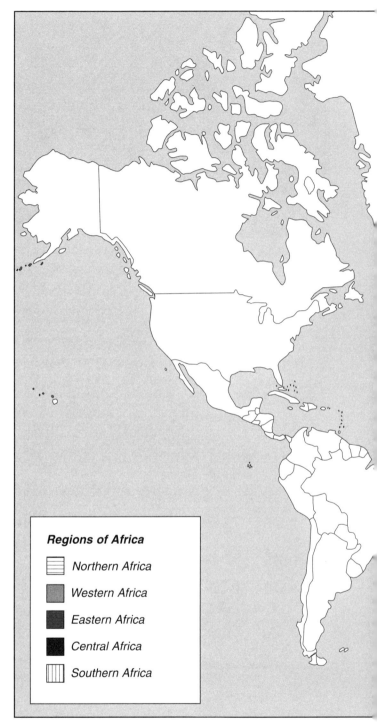

Regions of Africa

Northern Africa

Western Africa

Eastern Africa

Central Africa

Southern Africa

CHAPTER 1

Africa and Its People

Iwa ni csin.
"Character is religion."

This proverb of the Yoruba people of Nigeria, West Africa, expresses a fundamental truth about the character of the African people. When they are in need, they turn to superhuman powers for help. They address their prayers to God, either directly or indirectly, through lesser gods or spiritual go-betweens.

When they address God, the elders of the Gikuyu people of Kenya, for example, gather the people of the community together under a sacred tree. A procession arrives. At its head are two children. A boy carries a calabash, or gourd, filled with milk; a girl carries a calabash of honey-beer. A lamb follows them, and last come the elders. When the procession reaches the base of the sacred tree, the leading elder takes the calabashes from the children. Facing Mt. Kenya, he raises the calabashes and addresses God with the following prayer.

"Reverend Elder [God] who lives on Kere-Nyaga ['Mountain of Brightness,' which is the Gikuyu name for Mt.

■ **African Religion as Manifested by African Ethnicities**

Northern Africa
Obsolete Religions:

Berber Religion

Cushite Religion

Egyptian Religion

Eastern Africa
Obsolete Religion:

Aksumite Religion

Living Religions:

Dinka Religion

Nuer Religion

Shilluk Religion

Galla Religion

Acholi Religion

Ateso Religion

Baganda Religion

Bagisu Religion

Banyankore Religion

Langi Religion

Banyoro Religion

Lugbara Religion

Akamba Religion

Akikuyu Religion

Maasai Religion

Bahaya Religion

Bachagga Religion

Bafipa Religion

Bahehe Religion

Bamakonda Religion

Banyakyusa Religion

Basukuma Religion

Banyamwezi Religion

Central Africa
Living Religions:

Babemba Religion

Bacongo Religion

Baluba Religion

Bandembu Religion

Banyakyusa Religion

Baka Religion

Bambuti Religion

Shona Religion

Banyarwanda
Religion

Barundi Religion

Southern Africa
Living Religions:

!Kung Religion

Khoi Religion

Lovedu Religion

San Religion

Sotho Religion

Swazi Religion

Tswana Religion

Xhosa Religion

Zulu Religion

Western Africa
Living Religions:

Ashanti Religion

Bambara Religion

Dogon Religion

Edo Religion

Ewe Religion

Fang Religion

Fanti Religion

Fon Religion

Ga Religion

Igbo Religion

Mende Religion

Nupe Religion

Tiv Religion

Yoruba Religion

Kenya]. You who make mountains tremble and rivers flood; we offer you this sacrifice that you may bring us rain. People and children are crying; sheep, goats and cattle are crying. Mwene-Nyaga ['Possessor of Brightness,' the Gikuyu name for God], we beseech you, with the blood of this lamb, which we are going to sacrifice to you. Refined honey and milk we have brought for you. We praise you in the same way as our forefathers used to praise you under this very same tree, and you heard them and brought them rain. We beseech you to accept this, our sacrifice, and bring us rain of prosperity." The people respond, "Peace, we beseech you, Ngai, peace be with us."

More than 730,000,000 people live on the African continent. Many are at home in the bustling cities of the north—Cairo, Tripoli, Tunis, Algiers—where the religion today is predominantly Islam. Another large concentration of people is at the continent's southern tip, in South Africa, where Christianity has a strong foothold. But between these two developed areas lies the largest part of Africa, where many people live in communities that at least to some extent follow traditional ways of life that stretch back thousands of years.

Beginning in prehistoric times, the people of Africa gathered in groups related by family ties and similar needs. These communities developed their own individual languages, cultures, practices, and religions. Although waves of exploration and modernization have had their impact on the traditional African way of life, it is estimated that there are more than 6,000 different peoples in Africa today. Many of these people continue to live by the spiritual influence of their ancestral way of life. Even after they have left their native villages to live in the cities, most Africans still identify themselves according to the heritage of their ancestors. Around 108,300,000 African people continue to practice their native religions.

A Population of Believers

Statistics on religion available from 35 African nations (*Current World Leaders Almanac:* 1998) show that African religion is very much alive. Even those countries on the West African coast that have had a Christian missionary presence since the 15th century still have high percentages of adherents of African religion. In three of these countries, Liberia, Togo, and Benin, more than 70 percent of the people claim to be adherents of African religion. Burkina Faso, Guinea-Bissau, Madagascar, and Cameroon also have more than 50 percent. The rest of the

■ *The Adinkira*
The Ashanti people of Ghana in West Africa have developed a variety of Adinkira, designs that have symbolic meaning. These designs are often stamped on cloth known as Adinkira cloth and used for decoration. The Adinkira above is the Gye Nyame, which means "Except God [I fear none]." It expresses the supremacy of God.

■ African Countries with More than 50% of the Population Practicing African Religion	
Liberia	70%
Togo	70%
Benin	70%
Burkina Faso	65%
Guinea-Bissau	65%
Madagascar	52%
Cameroon	51%

African nation-states maintain percentages between 48 percent and 1 percent. Of the total population of religious adherents in Africa, 30 percent practice African religion. In addition, there are a sizable number of adherents in African-influenced religions in the Americas and elsewhere in the world. If numbers of adherents are indicative of the continued existence of a religion, then the numbers of adherents of African religion ensure its continuation in the future.

The African Continent

To understand African religion, it helps to look at Africa itself. Africa is the second largest continent on earth. Only Asia is larger. Africa's 11,700,000 square miles make it about three times the size of Europe, twice the size of the United States including Alaska. On the north, where it shares the waters of the Mediterranean Sea with Spain, Italy, and Greece, it lies close to Europe. Only the narrow Red Sea separates it from the Middle East. Its western shore stretches along the North and South Atlantic Ocean, and its eastern shore the entire length of the Indian Ocean.

Because of its vast size, Africa is a land of contrasts. It contains one of the world's greatest deserts, the Sahara, which stretches across the north-central part of the continent, dividing north from south. North of the Sahara lie countries rich with ancient tradition. Ancient Egypt, whose pharaoh once ruled vast holdings in the Middle East, was one of the most powerful countries in the world. Carthage, a great city-state centuries before the Roman Empire, lay in what is now Tunisia. Trading with Greece and Rome, and with Asia to the East, the North Africans developed cosmopolitan cultures. They built large cities, erected monuments, and developed written language. They worshiped their own ancient gods. Later, their traditional religions would be swept aside by Islam and to some extent by Christianity.

The Sub-Sahara

Below the Sahara is a land of enormous variety, from snow-covered mountains and deep valleys with great rivers to open grasslands to rainforest. Cut off from known civilization by the huge, empty Sahara, these lands remained largely untouched by outside exploration for centuries. But they were not uninhabited. Indeed, humanity as we know it may have sprung from deep within the African continent. Recent scientific studies in Kenya and elsewhere in Africa strongly suggest that Africa may be the birthplace of the human race.

African Peoples and Their Religions

Over many centuries, the African peoples below the Sahara lived in close harmony with the land. Some were nomads—wanderers—who followed the animals they hunted or established camps where their herds could graze. Others farmed or lived off the land, gathering native plants for food. Often they were widely separated from their closest neighbors. Living more or less in isolation, they developed their own languages and customs. They also developed religious practices that served their particular lives and needs.

African religion teaches that people are made up of moral, social, spiritual, and physical parts. These parts function together. If any part is out of balance, the person may become physically ill or suffer spiritually. That is why a conflict with another person may make someone sick, or a moral misdeed may bring about misfortune.

African religion is not the only religion found in Africa today. However, it is the only religion that can claim to have originated in Africa. Other religions found in Africa have their origins in other parts of the world.

African Religion and Other Religions

African religion differs from religions such as Judaism, Christianity, and Islam in a number of ways. Although individual peoples may remember legendary figures from their history, African religion has no single founder or central historical figure, such as Moses, Jesus, or Muhammad. Like Native American religions and Asian religions such as Shinto and folk Taoism, it originates with the people themselves. It is an expression of many thousands of years of living close to the land and of seeking answers to the mysteries of life: Why are we here? How do we live well? Why do we die?

African religion has no churches or mosques like those of Christianity or Islam. Instead, it has shrines constructed according to the traditions of the particular geographical area. People may also turn to a geographical or natural feature, such as a mountain or a large tree, as a focus for worship.

In African religion, there is no single ordained priesthood. Religious duties are carried out by a variety of religious leaders. There are priests and priestesses, healers, diviners, mediums, seers, rainmakers, elders, and rulers, each with a special role in maintaining the spiritual life of the community and its people.

The Oral Tradition

Traditional African lore has always been passed down orally. There is no written set of beliefs, no "holy book" such as the Bible or the Koran. Cultural beliefs and rules for living are passed down from generation to generation by word of mouth. Most African peoples have no written language, but members of the community are trained from childhood to perform prodigious acts of memorization, reciting the whole history of the community for untold generations.

Basic Beliefs

Followers of African religion make no distinction between religion and other aspects of their lives. Their beliefs are so closely bound to their culture that religion and culture are one. Religion is therefore not something people do at certain times and in certain places, but it is part of the fabric of living. Although the supreme God is above the living, lesser gods, spirits, and ancestors walk beside the living and guide them in the direction they must go. They are sometimes displeased by those who do not heed them. People and gods are constantly interacting through ritual, prayer, and sacrifice, but mostly through the business of living.

Although traditional African religion varies widely from region to region and people to people, there are a number of things that they all have in common.

- All things in the universe are part of a whole. There is no sharp distinction between the sacred and the nonsacred.
- There is a Supreme Being: a creator, sustainer, provider, and controller of all creation.
- Serving with the Creator are a variety of lesser and intermediary gods and guardian spirits. These lesser gods are constantly involved in human affairs. People communicate with these gods through rituals, sacrifices, and prayers.
- The human condition is imperfect and will always be so. Sickness, suffering, and death are all fundamental parts of life. Suffering is caused by sins and misdeeds that offend the gods and ancestors, or by being out of harmony with society.
- Ritual actions may relieve the problems and sufferings of human life, either by satisfying the offended gods or by resolving social conflicts. Rituals help to restore people to the traditional values and renew their commitment to a spiritual life.
- Human society is communal. Ancestors, the living, the living-dead, and those yet to be born are all an important part of the community. The relationships between the worldly and the otherworldly help to guide and balance the lives of the community. Humans need to interact with the spirit world, which is all around them.

Among African peoples, community, culture, and religion are tightly bound together. The African view of the world is fundamentally one of being part of a communal group. People believe in sharing their property and services, and they expect the other members of the community to share with them. They believe that "whatever happens to the individual happens to the whole group, and whatever happens to the group happens to the individual. The individual can only say, 'I am, because we are, and since we are, therefore I am.'" In this community spirit lies their security. (*African Religions and Philosophy*, pp. 108–109)

■ *A pyramid and Sphinx located in Giza, a suburb of Cairo, Egypt. The pyramid is an example of the symbols of ancient Egyptian religious life.*

Africa and Its History

Although much of Africa was isolated from the rest of the world, the areas along the coasts developed important cultures. By 3400 B.C.E., Egypt was a flourishing empire with a highly developed religion. The pyramids are its most visible and lasting testimony. But although they represent a triumph of technology, Egyptian pyramids are more than just great wonders of the world. They are also religious structures. Spiritually, pyramids are ritual objects that reflect the ancient connection of kingship to African religion, along with belief in life hereafter and immortality.

Egyptian religion was not the only ancient religion in ancient Africa. Judaism originated in the Middle East, but as early as 1300 B.C.E., groups of Hebrew peoples were living on the African continent, primarily in Egypt. In Ethiopia since biblical times, there have lived thousands of African Jews, known to Ethiopians as *Falashas*. These so-called Black Jews of Ethiopia practice a religion based entirely on the Old Testament of the Bible but including certain Ethiopian African religious elements. Like other Ethiopians they believe in and use amulets, charms, and magic ritual and prayers.

Early Christianity in Africa

According to Christian tradition, Mary and Joseph, the parents of Jesus Christ, fled to Egypt with the baby Jesus to escape persecution. So in one sense, Christianity came to Africa even before its founding. Some of the earliest Christian communities were in North Africa. When Christianity began its spread out of the Middle East, it moved into Greece, and from there to Greek colonies. Historians believe that Christianity first came into Africa around 40 C.E. through Alexandria, a city of the Hellenic Empire founded by Alexander the Great. At about the same time, a Christian community arose in Egypt that was made up of

■ *Nubian pyramid-tombs, under which the pharaohs and candaces of Meroe were buried. They signify ancient Nubian religion.*

native Egyptians. The Copts, a Christian sect, trace their origins to the preaching of St. Mark, one of the writers of the Christian Gospels, who visited Egypt.

A second way in which Christianity spread to Africans was through Carthage, a Roman province that lay in what is now Tunisia. From about 44 B.C.E. Carthage was culturally Roman; its official language was Latin. The official religion was worship of the Roman gods. Christians were persecuted and even killed. Persecution seems to have worked against the Romans, however, because Christianity grew rapidly in North Africa. African Christianity produced such great leaders as Tertullian, Saint Augustine, Saint Cyprian, and Saints Perpetua and Felicity. At least one writer, Tertullian, recognized the importance of the African religious concepts of God to developing Christianity. In 350 C.E., the ancient kingdom of Aksum, known as Ethiopia today, officially embraced Christianity. At that time, the Aksumite king Ezana, originally a strong adherent of his African religion, converted to Christianity. Aksumite Christianity, later called Ethiopian Christianity, has its roots in the Coptic Christianity of Egypt.

African Religion and Islam

"Islam" means "submission to the will of God." The creed of Islam is "There is no god but Allah [God], and Muhammad is His prophet." When Muslims arrived in Africa after the seventh century C.E., they did not identify African religion as a religion. They called the native people *kaffirs*, which means "infidels" — people who have no faith, or unbelievers. The name stuck, and Africans came to be known as people with no faith. The early Muslims did not wage a holy war against African religion, as they did in other countries, or practice forced conversions. However, Islam proved to be an attractive religion to many Africans, particularly in the north, who may have found similarities between their religion and Islam. Today, Islam is one of the most dynamic religions in Africa. It is well represented in practically all African nations. In some African countries it is the predominant religion.

■ *African Religion*	*Islam*
monotheistic	*monotheistic*
polytheism (associate gods)	*no secondary gods*
no division between sacred and secular	*no division between sacred and secular*
allows plural marriage	*allows plural marriage*
belief in afterlife	*belief in afterlife*

The Arrival of the Portuguese

The Portuguese came to Africa during the 15th century. Prince Henry the Navigator hoped to find a safe new access to Asia and Africa and their treasures, which included pepper, spices, gold, ivory, gems, jewelry, and metal. He received the blessing of the pope, who authorized Portugal and Spain to conquer and possess lands and their riches as well as to pass on the message of Christianity.

The expeditions usually included chaplains and priests. Sailing along the West and East African coasts, they preached the Christian message to the people they met and took advantage of African hospitality. Eventually they established African Christian communities. But they were to be disappointed. African peoples had welcomed them warmly. But that did not mean that they were ready to give up their cultures and beliefs. The missionaries failed to appreciate the African religion and culture on which the welcome was based, and misunderstanding arose. In frustration, the missionaries developed hostile attitudes toward the people. Finally they succumbed to the temptations of the slave trade. Portuguese-sponsored Christianity in Africa ended badly.

During the 19th century, European countries staked claims to African lands in the rush to build empires. This so-called "scramble for Africa" saw African countries divided among the British, the French, and the Dutch, among others. Overwhelmingly Christian, they invited a new wave of Christian missionaries, who

■ *The Dyanne mosque in Mali on market day.*

came bringing "missions Christianity" with them. Missionaries to Africa included not only Roman Catholic priests, as in the case of the Portuguese and Spanish, but also clerics and laypeople of various Protestant denominations.

The missionaries established schools and hospitals and began preaching the gospel of Christianity. They were well-meaning, but they had little understanding of the cultures they were entering. Their intent was to bring Christianity to a continent they believed to have no true religion. They meant to stamp out African religious practices they saw as superstition and ignorance.

Living and working among the African people, some members of missionary societies began to appreciate Africans and African religion. They began to make the effort to understand the culture. From this effort, they could finally begin to establish a Christian relationship with African religion.

Unity and Diversity in African Religions

Although it is possible to make some generalizations about African religion, it is important to remember that African religions are not one, but many. African religions have a great variety of rituals, myths, beliefs, and deities. Yet in spite of their differences from each other and from many other world religions, they share with each other and with most other faiths the goal of guiding individuals safely through the passages of life, from birth and puberty, marriage and maturity, to death and ancestorhood. They mark not only the seasons of life, each with its particular responsibilities and duties, but also the seasons of the year and the cycles of time. They answer the questions of why there is suffering and death in the world and offer ways of dealing with human pain. Finally, they provide a way for the people who follow them to be in touch with the spiritual in themselves and in the universe.

There are as many African religions as there are African peoples. But in their diversity, they are one. Whether African religion is based in Central Africa, Eastern Africa, Western Africa, or Southern Africa, the belief in the Supreme Being and the superhuman beings are its cornerstones. They point to the same understanding.

2

The Beginning of Time: The Oral Tradition

*A*frican peoples have wonderful tales to tell about the beginning of time. Traditionally, the elders of the village gather the children and tell them about times when the world was young, when animals could talk, when heroes walked among humankind, when God made the earth and everything in it. In the hands of the skilled storyteller, the characters come alive, and the children will never forget them. The stories are entertaining, but entertainment is not their primary goal. As they listen, the children are absorbing the myths and the culture of their community.

How Tradition Is Passed On

Living close to nature, Africans have always observed the world around them. Looking up, they saw the vast expanse of the sky. Around them they saw oceans, seas, lakes, rivers, forests, animals, and many other marvels of creation. They pondered the kinds of questions that humankind has asked for untold centuries. How did the world come to be? What hand fashioned us and put us here? What does it mean to be alive?

Over centuries, people formed answers to such questions, often in the form of stories, myths, and proverbs. These answers were passed down by word of mouth from one generation to the next. Thus are oral traditions, many of which address questions of existence from the beginning of time, established. The oral traditions constitute the method of transmitting history and religious traditions by spoken rather than written means. In African traditional communities, it was part of home education to memorize those traditions with great accuracy.

Oral traditions are passed on in a variety of forms—in myths, legends, stories, and proverbs. *Stories* in general say something about life for reasons of educating and entertaining the community. *Myths* deal with the divine. They have religious subjects, such as the origin of the universe and of nature. They address and answer questions like *Where did humankind come from? How are human beings expected to act as they travel through life? What is the destiny of the human race?*

Legends are a body of stories about families, people, and particularly heroes of the community. Often based on real people and facts, they have been told and retold until they become part of the lore of the community as a whole. *Proverbs* are short statements that express wisdom about creation and human experience.

Creation Myths and the Fall of Humankind

From their earliest beginnings, African people have asked questions about their existence. Such questions as *Who are we? How did we come to be here? How should we understand our place in this world?* have given rise to the rich and varied creation myths of African peoples.

Myths of creation tell of the sacred beginnings of the people. They usually center on a Supreme Being who, according to African oral tradition, is the creator of the world. They recognize the special position the Creator has given to humankind.

The following is an example of an African creation myth. It tells how the different stages of creation were carried out. It comes from the Yoruba people of Nigeria in West Africa.

In the beginning the world was a watery, formless Chaos that was neither sea nor land, but a marshy waste. Above it, in the sky, lived the Supreme Being, Olodumare (Olorun), attended by other gods, including Orisha Nla, called the Great God. Olodumare called Orisha Nla into his presence and ordered him to make a world. It was time to make solid land, and Orisha Nla was given a snail shell full of magic earth, a pigeon, and a five-toed hen to accomplish this assignment. Orisha Nla came down to this Chaos and set to work organizing it. He threw the magic earth into a small patch. The pigeon and the hen began to scratch in the magic earth, and they scratched until land and sea were entirely separated.

When Orisha Nla returned to the Supreme Being to report on his work, a chameleon was sent with him to inspect the job. The chameleon reported good things, and Olodumare, satisfied with the good report, dispatched Orisha Nla to finish. The first place on earth was known as "Ife," which means "wide" in the Yoruba language. Later, the word "Ile" meaning "house," was added. Today the city of Ile Ife is the most sacred to the Yoruba people.

The making of the earth took four days. On the fifth, Orisha Nla rested from his work. The Yoruba traditionally have a four-day work week and rest on the fifth in memory of creation.

Orisha Nla was sent back to earth to plant trees, including the first oil palm. Olodumare made the rain fall from heaven to water the seeds, which grew into a great forest. In heaven, Olodumare began to make the first people. They were fashioned from earth by Orisha Nla, but only Olodumare, the Supreme Being, could give them life. Orisha Nla hid in Olodumare's workshop to watch. However, Olodumare knew that Orisha Nla was hiding *there and put him into a deep sleep, and so only Olodumare knows the secret of how to bring a body to life. To this day, Orisha Nla, through the agency of parents, makes the body, but only the Supreme Being can give it life.*

African creation myths often tell about the special relationship between God and the first people, when the heavens were very close to earth. But humankind, being imperfect, made mistakes, for which they must be punished. The Dinka people say that once a rope hung down from heaven for people to climb up when they wanted to talk to God. But an old woman mashing yams kept hitting the underside of heaven with her pestle, and weary of the noise, God pulled up the rope and withdrew the heavens to a higher plane. Still, people are always encouraged to make up for their failures. African myths commonly conclude with a lesson about the importance of people living well in this world.

The following creation myth from the Barotse people of Zambia describes a time when God and the early humans

■ *Storytelling in Africa is not confined to oral language. It may also be done in dance. Here, Luo dancers from East Africa dramatize a national story.*

walked the earth together. But Kamonu, the first man, is literally too smart for his own good. He wants everything God has. Through the misbehavior of Kamonu, God withdraws from earth to reign in the heavens.

> In the beginning, Nyambi made all things. He made animals, fishes, birds. At that time he lived on earth with his wife, Nasilele. One of Nyambi's creatures was different from all the others. His name was Kamonu. Kamonu imitated Nyambi in everything Nyambi did. When Nyambi worked in wood, Kamonu worked in wood; when Nyambi forged iron Kamonu forged iron.
>
> After a while Nyambi began to fear Kamonu. Then one day Kamonu forged a spear and killed a male antelope, and he went on killing. Nyambi grew very angry at this. "Man, you are acting very badly," he said to Kamonu. "These are your brothers. Do not kill them."
>
> Nyambi drove Kamonu out into another land. But after a while Kamonu returned. Nyambi allowed him to stay and gave him a garden to cultivate. It happened that at night buffaloes wandered into Kamonu's garden and he speared them; after that some elands [antelope] came, and he killed one. After some time Kamonu's dog died; then his pot broke; then his child died. When Kamonu went to Nyambi to tell him what had happened he found his dog and his pot and his child at Nyambi's.
>
> Then Kamonu said to Nyambi, "Give me medicine [power] so that I may keep my things." But Nyambi refused to give him medicine. After this Nyambi met with his two counselors and said, "How shall we live since Kamonu knows too well the road thither?"
>
> Nyambi tried various means to flee Kamonu. He removed himself and his court to an island across the river. But Kamonu made a raft of reeds and crossed over to Nyambi's island. Then Nyambi piled up a huge mountain and went to live on its peak. Still Nyambi

could not get away from man. Kamonu found his way to him. In the meantime people were multiplying and spreading all over the earth.

Finally Nyambi sent birds to go look for a place for Litoma, god's town. But the birds failed to find a place. Nyambi sought council from a diviner. The diviner said, "Your life depends on Spider." And Spider went and found an abode for Nyambi and his court in the sky. Then Spider spun a thread from earth to the sky and Nyambi climbed up on the thread. Then the diviner advised Nyambi to put out Spider's eyes so that he could never see the way to heaven again and Nyambi did so.

After Nyambi disappeared into the sky, Kamonu gathered some men around him and said, "Let us build a high tower and climb up to Nyambi." They cut down trees and put log on log, higher and higher towards the sky. But the weight was too great and the tower collapsed. So that Kamonu never found his way to Nyambi's home.

But every morning when the sun appeared, Kamonu greeted it, saying, "Here is our king. He has come." And all the other people greeted him shouting and clapping. At the time of the new moon, men call on Nasilele, Nyambi's wife.

Heroes and Legends

Human life is generally marked by success and failure as well as a variety of minor ups and downs. Hero tales and legends focus on success, encouraging a positive group image. In African traditions, many heroes are human beings who are deified, that is, elevated to the status of gods. Through their acts on earth, they become associates of the Supreme Being. A hero may be someone who does a great deed for the community or someone who seems touched by the gods, especially chosen from childhood for some higher purpose.

■ *A Kikuyu elder. Among the Kikuyu people of Kenya, elders are not only heads of households, but also community ritual leaders. Here, an elder presides over a religious function.*

Lubaale Mukasa, a god of the Baganda people of East Africa, is an example of a deified hero, a human who has become a god. The title *lubaale* refers to a spiritual being.

Mukasa was the son of lubaale *Wannema, whose temple was on Bukasa Island in the Ssese Islands* [of the great Lake Victoria in East Africa]. *Before the birth of Mukasa, his mother, Nnambuubi, had refused to touch any food except a special kind of ripe plantains known as* gonja. *She would not eat cooked food. When the boy was born, he was given the name Sserwanga. When the boy was weaned, he refused to eat ordinary food. He ate the heart and liver of animals, and he drank their blood. While still a child, he disappeared from home. He left no traces behind him as to his whereabouts. Eventually he was found on the island of Bubembe, sitting under a large tree near the lake. Some people saw him as they passed the place. They told the elders of the village, who in turn went to see him and find out who he was. Their findings brought them to the conclusion that he had come from the island called Bukasa. So they referred to him as a Mukasa, that is, a person who originates on Bukasa Island. One of the men who went to see him, named Ssemagumba, told his companions that he could not leave the boy on the shore all night. So he carried him up to a garden and placed him upon a rock, until they could decide where he was to go. The people were afraid to take him to their houses, because they sensed that he must be superhuman to have thus come to their island. It was decided that a hut should be built for him near the rock on which he was seated, and that Ssemagumba should take care of him. They were at a loss as to what to give him to eat because he refused all sorts of things which they brought to him. They happened to kill an ox, and he at once asked for blood, the liver, and the heart, though he refused any of the meat which they offered him. This confirmed their opinion that he was a god.*

They consulted him about any illness. They sought his advice when they were in need or trouble. He was benign. He did not ask for the life of any human being. He had nothing to do with war. He was interested in healing the bodies and the minds of the people. He was consulted in matters of health, wealth, and fertility.

After Mukasa had disappeared as suddenly as he had come, he continued to be acknowledged as holding the highest rank among the gods of Buganda.

Stories and Fables

Stories and fables usually illustrate some truth about human nature and end with a stated or unstated moral. Such stories are partly for entertainment, but they are more than just amusing tales. They are the African way of teaching and passing down ethics, or right behavior, to the next generation.

One of the most famous African folk heroes is Ananse, the spider. Ananse is the hero of numerous folktales of the Akan people of West Africa. The Ananse tales have crossed from West Africa to the Americas, where they are familiar to many children. Ananse is a trickster. Tricksters may be human or animal or a little of both, but they all have superhuman powers that they can use for good or for harm. They also suffer from many of the character flaws that ordinary humans have, such as greed and envy. As a result, they are often caught in their own snares. Stories about Ananse, or as he is usually called, Father Ananse, attribute great skill and ingenuity to him. In this tale, Ananse tries to take back the wisdom he has distributed in the world, only to lose it to humankind.

Why Some People Have More Wisdom than Others

Once upon a time, there lived a man called Father Ananse in the village of "Nowhere." Ananse was acclaimed as the wisest man on earth because he possessed all the wisdom in the world. It looked like God (Nyame) gave all the wisdom to Ananse, for no one did anything right in the village of Nowhere without first seeking Ananse's advice, counseling, or direction.

At one time, some of Ananse's consultants became ungrateful to him. He therefore decided to retaliate against them for their unbecoming act. The most effective punishment Ananse thought of was to stop giving anyone advice and to repossess all the wisdom he had given out. Ananse's word was his bond. So the next morning, he went from house to house to gather all the people's wisdom, which he stored in a large pot.

After Ananse had collected and sealed all the wisdom in a pot, he was faced with the task of guarding the pot of wisdom around the clock. This took away all the time he could have used for some work. He therefore decided to hide the pot of wisdom on the top of a tree where no one could gain access to it.

While this was going on, Ananse's eldest son, called Ntikuma, had noticed his father's hardheartedness and atrocious plans to hide all the wisdom. He began to watch Ananse thereafter.

When Ananse sneaked out of the house at dawn with the pot of wisdom, Ntikuma followed him secretly. After walking far into the forest, Ananse stopped under a tall tree. It was at the top of this tree that he wanted to hide the pot of wisdom. Prior to climbing the tree, Ananse tied a rope under the rim of the pot so that it could hang from his neck. With the pot hanging in front of his stomach, Ananse tried to climb the tree. But all the attempts he made to climb failed, for the pot in front did not make it possible for him to attach his body to the tree, much less to get a good grip on the branches of the tree. When Ananse had almost despaired after his many unsuccessful attempts to climb, his son Ntikuma, who had been watching from behind a tree, shouted, "Father, don't you think it will be easy for you to climb the tree if you let the pot hang from your back?" Ananse, turning around angrily, said, "I thought I had collected all the wisdom in the world. But I realize that you still have some of the wisdom. That is why you have been able to give me a wise suggestion."

■ *The leopard, like the lion, symbolizes ritual power. Here, a bronze statue of a leopard represents a spiritual aspect of the kingdom of Benin in Nigeria.*

Ananse angrily climbed the tree with the pot hanging from his back as his son had suggested. When he reached the top of the tree, fuming Ananse intentionally dropped the pot, which fell on a rock under the tree. All the wisdom in the pot split asunder. News about the incident reached all villages, towns, and cities everywhere. People from all over the world rushed to the spot to collect some of the spilled wisdom. Those who reached there first got much of the wisdom. But those who reached there later got very little of the wisdom. That is why all over the world, some people are wiser than others.

Proverbs

The Nupe people of West Africa express God's being without end in the proverb "God will outlive eternity." Proverbs are

■ **Proverbs in African Society**

Proverbs teach reverence for and appreciation of authority, the realiza-tion that God the Creator is a supreme being, reverence for justice, human sympathy and fellow feeling among individuals, the ability to [turn away from] bitterness and learn from painful experiences, and the futility of envy and competitiveness. They help you to understand that if you twist the arm of justice, you twist the morals of the society. We cannot all hope to be like the maize [corn]. The maize has good luck all the time. It goes to the soil naked and returns with good luck with hundreds of children. Look at your five fingers. Are they equal? So are human beings. The old man is wise because he is in his second child-hood and, like a child, he is always ready to learn.

from *Proverbs of Africa: Human Nature in the Nigerian Oral Tradition,* by Ryszard Pachocinski. St. Paul, Minn.: A PWPA Book, 1996.

short sayings that express a recognized truth. Because people repeat them often, they are easy to remember. African people express their belief in God and his works through proverbs that remind them constantly of his power.

The Akan people of West Africa have many proverbs that are related to their creation myths. Their name for God is *Nyame,* which means "the Supreme Being," "the Shining One," "the Originator," and "first mover of everything." Here are some of the ways in which their proverbs depict him:

> "No one points out the Nyame to a child."
> "The earth is wide, but Nyame is chief."
> "All people are Nyame's offspring; no one is the offspring of earth."
> "Says Hawk: All Nyame did is good."
> "The order Nyame has settled, living people cannot subvert."
> "There is no by-pass to Nyame's destiny."
> "When the fowl drinks water, it shows it to Nyame."

African Religions and the Oral Tradition

The African oral tradition, with its myths, legends, stories, and proverbs, instills the important elements of religion and culture in the minds and hearts of the African people. The stories, myths, and tales that they hear and repeat from early childhood teach them about the ethics and beliefs of their community. From their oral literature, they learn why things are as they are and how life is to be lived on this earth. Perhaps most importantly, they learn of the power and majesty of God, the Supreme Being, and of their special relationship to him, their creator and giver of all life.

CHAPTER **3**

The Supreme Being

*I*n the Adinkira patterns of Akan art, there is a pattern that is called Gye Nyame, meaning "Except God." When it appeared on a Ghana postage stamp, it was called "The Omniscience of God," referring to God's quality of omniscience, or knowing all things. A stamp collector remarked: "How apt that an African country should be the first to remind the world of God's power [on a stamp]." "Except God" is an end of a proverb that goes, "No one saw the beginning, none shall see the end, except God." That is to say that no one saw the beginning of creation, and no one will see its end, *except* God.

African oral traditions have always pointed to the existence of a power above which there is no other power, a supreme being, creator, and originator of the world. People who follow traditional African religion understand the Supreme Being to be one and only one, God with a capital "G."

The African Concept of Monotheism

In Western religion, religious systems are usually classified as either *monotheistic,* that is, believing in one God, or *polytheistic,* believing in many gods. In African religion, monotheism and

polytheism exist side by side. For a long time, scholars thought that African religion had always been polytheistic only. They thought that the Supreme Being of African religion was the result of contact with Christianity and Islam. We now know that this is not the case. The African concept of one supreme God existed well before Judaic, Christian, or Islamic influence.

Long before Judaism appeared on the scene around the second millennium B.C.E., long before Christianity appeared on the scene during the first century C.E., and long before Islam appeared on the scene in 641 C.E., African people believed in the Supreme Being. Moreover, the Supreme Being of African religion is what those other religions refer to as God in a monotheistic sense.

The African concept of monotheism is one of a hierarchy, with the Supreme Being at its head. In this system, the Supreme Being rules over a vast number of divinities who are considered to be the associates of God. African understanding of the structure of the heavenly kingdom might be compared to the Christian concept of God ruling over the saints and angels. The divine hierarchy in African religion makes it possible to classify them as both monotheistic and polytheistic at once (*monotheism with polytheism*).

God in One, Two, or Four

From time immemorial, African people have pondered the nature of the Supreme Being, whom they recognize as God. The result is a multisided idea of God. How the many different African peoples conceive of God usually follows the social structure of a particular locality or culture. African people whose cultures are organized as monarchies with a king at the head usually conceive of God as the supreme king. As there can be only one supreme king in a community, Africans have traditionally concluded that there can be only one supreme being for the entire human race.

Although God is one and one only, in African tradition, this uniquely one Supreme Being may be understood as being one in *unity,* or as one in *duality,* or as one in *quarternity*—that is, one in one, two in one, or four in one. The African concept of a single God having multiple being is similar to the Christian doctrine of God as a trinity, or three in one—father, son, and holy spirit.

The majority of African peoples conceive of God as one. However, among the Fon people of Benin in West Africa, *Nana-Buluku,* the name for God, expresses one God in *duality,* or two. In the Fon religion, God is two beings, male and female.

The most complex concept of God is that of the Bambara people of West Africa. The Supreme God of the Bambara is called *Bemba* or *Ngala.* Bemba has, in a way, created himself as a *quarternity.* The four aspects of Bemba are Bemba, Nyale, Faro, and Ndomadyiri. The Bambara people understand these aspects of their God to be pure creative energy that is expressed as four "persons." Each plays a different role in the creation of the universe.

Attributes of God

People in African religious traditions associate the Supreme Being with certain basic attributes. These are:

- God is the Creator of all things.
- God is the absolute controller and sustainer of the universe.
- God provides for what he created.
- God possesses all that he created.

The Creator of All Things

Both African oral traditions and later written sources indicate that all African peoples believe that power of creation is the foremost attribute of the Supreme Being. African myths of creation support the idea that all Africans at all times have recognized the Supreme Being as the Creator of all things. In addition, the names by which many different groups across Africa call the Supreme Being express the idea of God as the "Originator," creator of everything.

The Banyarwanda of Rwanda in Central Africa speak simply of creation by saying, "There was nothing before God created the world." In the same region, the Baila of Zambia call God "Creator." The Baila name is derived from the verb that means "to make," "originate," "to be the first to do anything." So God is thought of as the originator of all things. The Ngoni people of Southern Africa call God as creator, "The Original Source," and the Zulu of South Africa believe that God "made all things"; pointing to heaven they say, "the Creator of all things is in heaven." The Banyankore of Uganda in Eastern Africa refer to God as "the Creator who sets things in order, creates everything and gives new life," while the Akan of Western Africa refer to God as "He who alone created the world."

Controller and Sustainer of the Universe

In African tradition and thought, God has absolute control of the universe and all that it contains. This is because all other beings exist because of him. As Originator of the universe, God is the ultimate fountainhead of all power of all natural rules for orderly existence.

Peoples of the different regions of Africa express God's controlling and sustaining role of creation in various ways. The Ashanti of Ghana in West Africa regard God as the "Supreme

■ *Memorial head of an Oba, or a Benin king of Nigeria. Kings in Africa are also religious leaders. A relic or statue of a king is esteemed as a ritual object, as is this brass sculpture.*

Being, upon whom men lean and do not fall." The Nandi of Kenya in Eastern Africa believe that God "is the far-off driving force behind everything, the balance of nature." The Bambuti of Congo in Central Africa express the control and sustenance of God in the saying, "If God should die, the world would also collapse," which expresses their belief in the controlling and sustaining power of God. From South Africa the Zulu say that God "made us, and is, as it were, in us his work. We exist because He existed."

■ *Snow-covered Mt. Kilimanjaro is the highest mountain on the African continent. Such mountains, including Kenya, Elgon, Cameroon, and the Rwenzoli Range, are regarded as seats of divinity.*

The Provider

In names, in mythology, in legends, and particularly in proverbs, African people show that they are aware that God provides for them. They acknowledge this in a variety of ways.

The name for God among the Ovimbundu of Southwestern Africa means "He who supplies the needs of his creatures." In

expressing the basis of God's providence, the Baganda of Uganda in Eastern Africa have a proverb: "God gives his gifts to whosoever he favors." Africans have also observed that the providence of God functions entirely independently of human beings. The Ewe of Ghana in Western Africa say that God "is good, for he has never withdrawn from us the good things which he gave us"; the name by which the Bakiga know God means "the One who gave everything on this earth and can also take it away."

The Possessor of All He Created

In African thought, God is not only the giver of life, he is also the possessor of whatever has been created. The Barundi of Central Africa have two names that describe God as "the Owner of everything" and "the Owner of all powers." The Baganda of Uganda in Eastern Africa call God "the Master of all things." The Nuer of Sudan neither grumble nor complain when a person or a cow dies, but simply say that God "has taken only what was his own."

The Supreme Being in African Belief

Although they may pray and sacrifice to many lesser gods, African people hold the Supreme Being in special regard as the great creator and giver of life. The Supreme Being alone is the originator of the world and all that is in it, and it is to him that they owe their existence and the well-being of their communities. African people may interact spiritually with many gods, spirits, and ancestors, but in the world of spirits, there is only one God, the Supreme Being, who lives and reigns in heaven and whose creative power fills the universe.

■ The Names of God

The following names of God express African ideas of the One God the Creator. These African names demonstrate the unity of thinking about God while at the same time expressing the African diversity of expression about the same and one God. The names listed are all taken from Africa south of the Sahara Desert, where living African religion is found. They represent different regions, countries, and ethnicities.

Central African Regions

Country	Ethnicity	Name	Meaning
Burundi	Barundi	Imana	The Creator of everything
Cameroon	Bamum	Njinyi	He who is everywhere He who sees and hears everything
	Bulu	Mabee	The One who bears the world
	Duala	Ebasi	Omnipotent Father
Central African Republic	Baya	Zambi	Creator
Congo (Brazzaville)	Vili	Nzambi	Creator and ultimate source of power
Congo (Kinshasa)	Baluba	Vidye	Great Creator Spirit
Gabon	Fang	Nyame	Creator
Rwanda	Banyarwanda	Imana	The Creator of everything

Central African Regions (continued)

Country	Ethnicity	Name	Meaning
Zambia	Ambo	Leza	Creator
	Barotse	Nyambi	Creator
	Baila	Leza	Creator

Eastern African Regions

Country	Ethnicity	Name	Meaning
Kenya	Akamba	Mumbi	Creator, Maker, Fashioner
Sudan	Nuer	Kwoth	Creator Spirit
	Dinka	Jok	Creator Spirit
	Shilluk	Juok	Creator Spirit
Tanzania	Chagga	Ruwa	Sun
	Gogo	Mulungu	Creator
	Nyakyusa	Kyala	Owner of all things
	Bazinza	Kazooba	Power of the Sun
Uganda	Baganda	Katonda	Creator, Originator
	Alur	Jok	Creator Spirit
	Banyankore	Ruhanga	Creator and Fixer of everything

■ *The Names of God (continued)*

Western African Regions

Country	Ethnicity	Name	Meaning
Benin	Fon	Nana-Buluku	Original Creator
		Mawu-Lisa	Continuer of Creation
Burkina Faso	Tallensi	Wene	Sky God
Côte d'Ivoire	Akan	Onyankopon	Alone, the Great One
Gambia	Serer	Rog	Creator
Ghana	Ashanti	Nyame	The Shining One
Nigeria	Igbo	Chwuku	Great Spirit
	Yoruba	Olodumare	The Most Supreme Being
Senegal	Serer	Rog	Creator
Sierra Leone	Mende	Leve	The High Up One
	Kono	Yataa	The One you meet everywhere

The Names of God (continued)

Southern African Regions

Country	Ethnicity	Name	Meaning
Angola	Bacongo	Nzambi	Creator
	Ovimbundu	Suku	He who supplies the needs of His creatures
Botswana	Tswana	Modimo	The Greatest Spirit
Lesotho	Basuto	Molimo	The Greatest Spirit
Malawi	Chewa	Mulungu	The Creator
	Ngoni	Uluhlanga	The Original Source
South Africa	Zulu	Unkulunkulu	The Great Oldest One
Swaziland	Swazi	Mvelamqandi	"Who-appeared-first" The power above, unapproachable, unpredictable, of no specific sex
Zimbabwe	Shona	Mwari	He who is in, or owns the sky, the Great One of the Sky
	Ndebele	Unkulunkulu	The Great Oldest One

CHAPTER 4

The Spirit World

*I*n African religion, the Supreme Being reigns as God in heaven. However, in most traditions, he is not involved in the day-to-day affairs of human beings. This function he delegates to the less important gods of African belief who occupy the spirit world. The spirit world is made up of *superhuman beings*, beings of God's creation that occupy the spiritual universe between God and humanity, the space between heaven and earth. They invisibly tread the earth, so that they are continually present. It is to these lesser gods that people turn in times of joy and sorrow. It is to them that they make requests concerning their needs and desires, and to them that they make offerings and sacrifices for health and happiness, successful crops, the birth of healthy children, and protection from evil.

Superhuman beings exist in a hierarchy. That is, they are ranked according to their nearness and importance to the Supreme Being. The most important superhuman beings may be called *associates of God*. These are lesser gods who rank below the Supreme Being but who often work in concert with him. Other

influential spirits of the community are *intermediaries, guardians,* and *ancestors.* Intermediaries are spirit agents that act as go-betweens between divinities and humans. Spiritual guardians and ancestors are protectors and advocates for humans, spiritually positioned between superhuman beings and human beings.

Spirits of the Spirit World

African tradition and thought consider spirits to be elements of power, force, authority, and vital energy underlying all existence. Invisible though this power may be, Africans perceive it directly. People know and believe that spirits are there. In their daily lives they point to a variety of actions that verify the existence of spirits. They also know that spirits are to be handled with care. Hence the variety of rituals and taboos that acknowledge the existence of spirits.

Spirits are found everywhere. And where they are considered to be, people feel their presence. There is no object or creature, there is no corner of the earth, that is not inhabited by spirits. The more something commands awe—by its size, beauty, or power—the more that thing becomes identified with spirits.

Spiritual Guardians

Spirits, no matter at which level they may be, inspire some sense of superhumanity. One example of this is those spirits designated as *spiritual guardians.* Spiritual guardians are a varied group. Among them are ancestors and the spirits of departed heroes. Another type of spirit resides in natural landmarks. A nearby mountain may be the abode of the spirit that is guardian to the community. The spirit of a river may be identified as guardian of that area. An extraordinarily huge tree in a village may be considered the abode of a local spiritual guardian. Animal life, too, may house spirits. A leopard may be accepted in a community, not as a mascot, but as a spiritual anchorage of the guardian spirit of a locality. Guardian spirits of a community are identified in numerous ways. They become a focus of communal ritual. For example, the Galla people of Ethiopia and

Kenya in East Africa call on spiritual guardians of the community for protection against enemies with the following prayer:

> *If enemies would come,*
> *let not your small worm die,*
> *but stretch your hand over him.*

Spirits of the Departed

The spirits of the dead are part of the spirit world. Some are ancestors, and others are the spirits of the ordinary dead, that is, the dead of the community who are neither ancestors nor identified as outstanding members of the community. Africans do not worship their dead ancestors, but they do venerate and respect them. The ordinary dead are respected as well, with due ritual observations by all the members of the community. In African religious belief, when a person dies, his or her soul separates from the body and changes from being a soul to being a spirit. Becoming a spirit is a social elevation. What was human becomes superhuman. At this point the spirit enters the state of immortality. The living are expected to take note of this development and render due respect to the departed through ritual. Among the spirits of the departed are the ranking superhuman beings that form the mainstay of African polytheism.

People expect ancestors to be unceasing guardians of the living. The Edo people of Nigeria bury their dead with their feet pointing west, that is, toward the Ughoton, the old port of Benin on the West African coast. From there, the dead are believed to embark in canoes and cross the sea to the spirit world that lies in the dome of the sky. Senior family members speak prayers at the burial. One such prayer is the following:

> *Your children whom you have left here,*
> *you should order money for them.*
> *You should send them children.*
> *You should send them everything*
> *That is used in the world . . .*
> *As they have lived to do this for you.*
> *Let their children live to do it for them. . . .*

A medium from Buddu province in the kingdom of Buganda is seated between two paddles. The paddle is the symbol of Mukasa, the god of the great lake Naluballe, also known as Lake Victoria, the second largest lake in the world. The medium is dressed in full regalia embellished by cowrie shells, symbolizing sacredness. He holds a multiple-headed smoking pipe that rests on a drum. At his right foot is a calabash with a drinking straw, containing a ritual drink.

As you looked after your children
When you were in the world,
So you should look after them
Unceasingly.

African Polytheism

The term *polytheism* is derived from two Greek words: *polus*, meaning "many," and *theos*, "god." With regard to African religion, it means a system of belief that recognizes and venerates many gods. These are the *gods* with a lowercase "g" who are also described as associates of God with a capital "G." Not all African religion centers on the worship of many gods, but many, if not most, do.

The Spiritual Hierarchy

Imagine the universe as being like a government. At the head is the Creator, the Supreme Being. He is ever present, but does not manage the daily affairs of human beings. This responsibility he delegates to his associates—also divine, but of a lesser order. The associates of God are spiritually made to head departments. These gods have been brought into being as functionaries in the God-centered government of the universe. They are the divinities who do the spiritual work of managing the human world, and they are the ones people call on in times of trouble. They are local gods, intimately connected with local situations. Each of them is the god of a particular people with a specific function in ordering the total life of the community. Under their various names and functions, the divinities form the pantheon of gods in each particular locality. *Pantheon* is the term for all the gods of a particular people taken together. The pantheons of the different African religions differ somewhat according to the needs and character of the people.

The Yoruba Pantheon: Orisa

The Yoruba are a Nigerian ethnic group of 12 million people with a rich religious tradition. At the top of their religious ranking is Olodumare, the Supreme Being. Next are the associates of God known as divinities, gods, or deities. These are ranked according to the importance of the function they oversee. Next are the spirits of ancestors and those of the ordinary dead.

The pantheon of Yoruba gods is known as the *Orisa*. It has a membership of as many as 1,700 divinities. Examples of a few of the most important follow.

Orisanla

Orisanla, or, as he is sometimes called, Obalata, is the second in command in the Yoruba pantheon. Yoruba tradition refers to Orisanla as the offspring of Olodumare. He has many of Olodumare's attributes, and Olodumare has delegated creative powers to him. As Olodumare's deputy, he created the earth and its arrangement, as well as the physical part of human beings. For that reason he is called the "Maker."

Orunmilla

Orunmilla is the Yoruba god of *divination*, the practice of seeking to discover future events or hidden knowledge in one's life by consulting the superhuman world. The Yoruba believe that Olodumare has endowed Orunmilla with special wisdom and foreknowledge, so anyone wishing to know the future may consult Orunmilla through his priest, known as a *babalawo*. Yoruba tradition provides divination in a form known as *Ifa*, which Yoruba religious devotees consult before undertaking anything important.

Esu

Esu is the most complex of the Orisa. He contains both good and evil properties.

Esu's function is primarily that of a "special relations officer" between heaven and earth. He is the "inspector general" who reports to Olodumare on the actions of other divinities and those of human beings. Esu investigates, checks, and reports on the correctness of worship and sacrifices. Because of his assignment as inspector, Esu may be found everywhere, checking on the spiritual orderliness of the community.

Esu's dual nature of good and evil, together with the role of corresponding as mediator between heaven and earth, makes him a "trickster" figure, a kind of mischievous superhuman being. He is believed to hold power of life and death, depending on the kind of reports he makes to Olodumare. Consequently, Yoruba people seek to be on good terms with him. They venerate him whenever they venerate any other Orisa. Because of this, Esu has a place in every shrine.

People strive to be on good terms with Esu by being constantly vigilant. They try to avoid anything that may annoy him. For example, should some mishap occur, they are quick to make good what may have gone wrong. They also make sure that Esu's portions of sacrifices are duly offered to him.

Ogun

Ogun is another associate of God who ranks high in the Yoruba pantheon. He is the divinity of war and of iron. Ogun exists on the edge of society. He is as hard and tough as steel, and all iron and steel are his spiritual possessions. He rules over oaths, covenant-making, and the cementing of pacts. In local courts, instead of swearing "to speak the truth and nothing but the truth," by holding the Bible or the Koran, Yoruba people take oaths by kissing a piece of iron, usually a machete, in recognition of Ogun's spiritual authority.

Ogun is recognized as the patron of warriors, hunters, artisans, blacksmiths, goldsmiths, engineers, mechanics, barbers,

■ *A staff that, according to the religion of the Yoruba people of Nigeria, symbolizes Sango, the god of thunder and lightning.*

butchers, truck and taxi drivers, and ironworkers of all kinds. Such people often visit Ogun's shrine in search of spiritual assurances for their work.

Jakuta and Sango

The expression "the Wrath of God" is represented by the gods Jakuta and Sango. Jakuta is one of the lesser divinities of heaven, whereas Sango is believed to have once been a human being who was raised to the status of a divinity. Jakuta literally means "the one who fights with stones" or "the one who hurls stones," and originally the commandments against stealing, falsehood, and poisoning were his.

Jakuta and Sango are regarded as coworkers in creating lightning and thunder. The Yoruba have such a sense of God's wrath that during a thunderstorm, people who have reason to fear God begin to tremble. It is in this sense that Yoruba tradition regard Jakuta and Sango as being functionaries of God's ministry of justice.

The Baganda Pantheon: Lubaale

The Baganda are an ethnic group of Uganda. Their pantheon is called *Lubaale,* or beings from *Olubaale,* the dome of the sky. It contains about 70 divinities. They know the Supreme Being as Katonda, which means "Creator." The Baganda speak of Katonda as the father of the gods, because he created all things. While some Baganda divinities are connected to nature, the majority of them are hero or ancestor gods who have been raised to the status of divinity.

Ggulu

Literally, *Ggulu* means "sky," "heaven." It is the name both of heaven and of the sky god. Ggulu is thus the divinity next to Katonda, the Supreme Being. In Buganda lore, the wife of the founder of the Buganda kingdom was the daughter of Ggulu, who came to earth from heaven with her brother Walumbe. The Buganda people originate with her, and therefore from heaven.

Kiwanuka

Kiwanuka means "something that descends at a great speed." Kiwanuka is god of thunder and lightning. He is also a god of fertility whom couples consult when they wish to have a child. When their prayers are successful, parents often name their child for the god: Kiwanuka for a son, or Nakiwanuka for a daughter.

Kitaka

Kitaka is believed to be the Mother Earth. The king consulted this divinity in cases of capital punishment so that the spirits of the dead might not return to harm him. People also consult Kitaka about cultivating the land, in order to have abundant crops.

Walumbe

The literal translation of this god's name is "Mr. Death." Walumbe is the son of Ggulu, the sky god, and the brother-in-law of Kintu, the first king of Buganda. When Walumbe's sister, the king's wife, made a mistake of forgetting to bring some provisions to earth and went back to the sky to fetch them, Walumbe, her brother, returned to earth with her. Since then Mr. Death has lived in the underworld as the divinity of death. A temple to him, built and cared for at Tanda in Uganda, reminds the population of the existence of death.

Wanga

Wanga is one of the oldest of the population of the deified heroes of the Baganda. These "terrestrial gods," lower ranking than the "sky gods" who rule in heaven, are the ones to whom the Baganda turn on a daily basis with their prayers and concerns. In the traditions of the Baganda people, the Sun once fell from the sky. The king called upon Wanga. He rose to the challenge and restored the Sun in its place in the heavens. As a reward, the king allotted an estate to Wanga and built a temple there. People consult Wanga about sickness and disease. He also foretells how people may turn aside common calamities and troubles that befall communities.

Musisi

Musisi is the son of Wanga. His name means "earthquake." People turn to him during natural calamities such as earthquakes.

■ A mask of the Basonge people of the Democratic Republic of Congo. Such masks are used to keep wayward people of the community in line.

Mukasa

Mukasa is a deified hero of the Baganda. Of all the super-human beings within the lubaale who invisibly populate the earth and are in daily contact with humans, he ranks highest.

Mukasa is the god to whom people turn with concerns for health and fertility.

Kibuuka

Kibuuka, the brother of Mukasa, is the war god of the Baganda. Consultation regarding warfare and national defense is directed to him, together with his nephew Nende, also a divinity of war.

The Fon Pantheon: Vodun

The Fon pantheon is known as the Vodun. *Vodun* may mean god in the sense of a divinity, and it may also mean a pantheon. Vodun worship is the religion of the Dahomey, or Fon, people. All of the Fon gods are members of the Vodun, including the dead, who are elevated to the level of gods. The Vodun includes both the great gods and also lesser gods who stem from the greater pantheon.

The great gods are included in three pantheons. These are the Sky Pantheon, the Earth Pantheon, and the Thunder Pantheon. The Supreme Being of the Fon, *Nana-Buluku*, rules over all as the Originator, Creator of the beginnings of the universe. Priests of the Fon religion teach that Nana-Buluku was at once both male and female. This Creator is also believed to be the parent of *Mawu-Lisa*.

The Sky Pantheon: Mawu-Lisa

Mawu-Lisa is a complex god whose most striking feature is a dual nature. This twin god was born to Nana-Buluku, the Creator, who also represents the duality of female and male. Mawu is female, associated with aspects of the world that relate to the earth, the west, the Moon, the night, and the rising Sun. Lisa is male, representing the sky, the east, the Sun, the day, and the setting Sun.

In addition to representing the dualities of the physical world, Mawu-Lisa symbolizes opposing aspects of human life. Mawu, the female principle, reflects fertility, motherhood, gentleness, and forgiveness. Lisa, the male principle, reflects strength and toughness. Mawu-Lisa express together the unity and duality of the physical world.

The Earth Pantheon: Sagbata

The deity Sagbata is known as the "king of the earth." Sometimes he is referred to as the "owner of the soil." According to tradition, veneration of Sagbata arose after an epidemic of smallpox. Thus Sagbata came to be the divinity who protects against smallpox.

The Thunder and the Sea Pantheon: Sogbo

To the people of Benin the sea, thunder, and lightning present mysterious forces that are looked at in terms of superhuman powers. Therefore anything to do with thunder and the sea is addressed through the pantheon whose head is Sogbo.

The Fon Pantheon of Lesser Gods

Among the Fon pantheon of lesser gods, the most notable include Legba, the divine trickster; Se, the souls of man; Fa, fate and divination; and Da, the cult of the serpent. Legba was the youngest of the 12 children of Mawu-Lisa. When they divided the universe among their offspring, there was no domain left for Legba. Instead, they gave Legba the role of messenger between his siblings and parents. Legba's domain is therefore communication. Nothing happens without his awareness.

An Ifa tray. This is a decorated tray used in the divination ritual known as Ifa, related to the practice of using mystical means to discover hidden knowledge. Ifa is connected to the worship of Orunmilla, the god of oracles. Usually a picture of Orunmilla is included among the decorations on the tray.

Importantly, Legba conveys the wishes and desires of human beings to the Vodun.

People sacrifice to Legba, fearing that if he does not receive the sacrifices he demands, he can prevent the Vodun from hearing their supplications. But they also mistrust him, and they may hold him responsible for the misfortunes of life. They also characterize him as a trickster. However, Legba is an important figure in determining the fortunes of human beings, who can normally approach Mawu-Lisa only through him.

African Peoples and the Spirit World

Associates of God, natural spirits, the spirits of departed heroes, ancestors, and other members of the community all join together to create a sense of living in a spiritually charged universe. For African believers, the spirit world is never very far away. It is present in sky and sea, earth and all creation, and in the memory of those who have gone before. People feel communion with the spirits all around them and communicate with them regularly, through sacrifice, offering, worship, and simple conversation. The gods of African religion are as near to them as their family, friends, and neighbors.

CHAPTER **5**

Rites and Ritual in African Religion

*T*o Africans, belief without ritual action would take away much of religion's natural power. Rites and ritual punctuate all aspects of African religious life. Religion is so deeply ingrained in the daily life of traditional Africa that it is all but impossible to separate it from other aspects of the culture. In an African community, religion is the strongest influence upon people's thoughts, acts, and lives. Rites of passage and other communal rites are the clearest examples of how religion permeates all aspects of African life.

Rites of Passage

Rites of passage are rites that have to do with the human life cycle. They are practices, customs, and ceremonies that people perform to move people smoothly through the stages of life from beginning to end. These stages include birth and childhood, puberty and initiation, marriage, aging, and death.

Birth and Childhood

The early stages of the life cycle include conception, the period of pregnancy, the actual birth of the child, its naming, and

its childhood. The rites of birth begin with the pregnancy of the mother. The conception of a child is itself a mystery that holds religious wonder. It is part of the continuation of God's activity of creation. Some African traditions regard conception as a cooperative venture between the parents-to-be, God, and the associate gods. A tradition of the Banyarwanda and Barundi of Central Africa illustrates the idea of God's participation in conception. They have a custom and rite known in their language as *Amazi y'Imana*, which means "God's water." They keep a little water in the house at night. Every woman who hopes to bear a child will not go to bed without seeing to it that the water is there. Starting from the moment of conception, *Imana,* or God, is supposed to use the water in his work of creation.

The religious reliance on God and other superhuman powers only becomes more important when a couple fails to achieve conception. Then they turn to the designated divinities in charge of fertility. The couple and their supporters approach the divinities with prayers and sacrifices as a means of requesting the favor of pregnancy. When the favor is granted and the woman announces that she is pregnant, there is rejoicing. Both spiritual and medical precautions are taken to ensure normal pregnancy and delivery. Those involved offer a sacrifice to the Supreme Being, the national gods, or the ancestors and guardian spirits, who have an interest in seeing that the community continues through the birth of new members.

Pregnancy

African people consider a pregnant woman to be chosen for a duty—motherhood—that is a sacred calling. She is, therefore, subject to a variety of taboos. A *taboo* is the custom of putting someone or something under prohibition. The pregnant woman is encouraged and sometimes instructed to refrain from various activities. Some taboos have to do with her diet. During pregnancy, women are forbidden salt, because it may harm the child's skin. Eggs and pork are also taboo for reasons of protecting the child's appearance and shape. Other taboos regulate the woman's personal habits on religious grounds or for reasons of checking her sexual behavior. All are aimed at bringing about the safe birth of the child.

When the time for the birth comes, experienced elderly women act as midwives to help the mother to deliver the child. The role of midwife is considered the sacred calling of a medicine woman. In African religion, healing is a religious activity. The birth may take place in the house or nearby in a secure area of the garden.

Along with the newborn baby, the placenta and umbilical cord receive special consideration. These two items, so closely related to the newly born, require religious care. The ritual disposal of the placenta and the umbilical cord indicates that the child has died to the state of pregnancy and is now alive in another state of existence. The child is born into the new life as part of human society.

The Baganda of Uganda believe that a child is born with a double, or twin, called a *mulongo*. This twin consists of the placenta and umbilical cord. After the birth, the mother wraps the placenta in banana leaves and buries it at the foot of a banana tree in such a way as to protect it from wild animals. The tree then assumes sacred significance until the fruit matures. When the bananas ripen, the child's paternal grandmother uses them to prepare a sacred feast marking the occasion.

In addition, the mother preserves the part of the umbilical cord that remains attached to the child after birth. It is believed to contain a protective spirit. When it drops off, she wraps it in bark-cloth and preserves it. At the time of the child's naming, it is dropped in a container of banana wine, milk, and water. If it floats, the child is considered legitimate, and the naming proceeds. If the cord sinks, the child is considered illegitimate, and the mother is disciplined.

Naming the Child

The name a child receives is expected to express the very essence of the person who bears it. Names individualize children, give them a standing, and incorporate them into the community. Parents take much care, therefore, in name-giving.

Naming ceremonies in Africa differ from people to people, but the names themselves have a number of things in common. All African names have specific meanings. Most African personal names, at least indirectly, reflect religious belief. Some have strongly religious themes. There are countless personal names in African religious traditions that express religious themes. Some are connected with divinities and many are related to spiritual and human circumstance. Others relate to attributes of the

■ *African religion richly marks transitions from one life stage to another with ritual celebrations. Here, a ceremony marks the initiation of Bambuti boys from juniors to young adults.*

Supreme Being. For instance, the Luo-speaking people of Kenya, Sudan, Tanzania, and Uganda frequently name children Ojok, related to Jok, or "God." The Igbo parents of Nigeria honor Chukwu, that is, God, by naming their children in praise of his power.

Puberty and Initiation

Puberty rites are ceremonies performed to mark the time during which young people move from childhood to adolescence. They initiate young people into the adult world, marking the physical changes that signal the transition from the asexual world of childhood to the sexual world of adulthood.

The approach, timing, and places for the rites of initiation vary from people to people. Young people may be initiated either through physical initiation or through instructional retreats. Physical initiation usually means circumcision, or the removal of the foreskin of the penis for boys, and an operation to remove the clitoris for girls, although this practice is being abandoned by some cultures. Most important as far as initiation is concerned are the instructions that are carried out during the retreats.

Apart from their drama and impact, initiation rites convey many religious meanings. Elders take young people to retreats away from home where they learn the arts of communal living. They are introduced to the basic facts of adult life. They are taught the sharing of privileges, rights, duties, and responsibilities of the community. The initiation rites give them instruction in matters of sexual life, marriage, procreation, and family responsibilities. Through this initiation they are prepared as adults to shed blood for their people. They are also encouraged to accept the responsibility of planting their biological seed as a way of contributing toward a new generation of the community through marriage.

Marriage

Marriage is a starting point for a new generation, as it is a starting point for personal immortality through offspring. In African thought, marriage is a religious obligation. Without marriage there is no assurance of having descendants. The departed count on being taken care of by, and are assured of being reincarnated or reborn through, their descendants. A person who has no descendants, in effect, disrupts the chain of reincarnation, to the great annoyance of the superhuman beings. Marriage, therefore, is a sacred undertaking that must not be neglected.

Aging

As they advance in age, people are deemed to grow in experience and wisdom. Parents are expected to bear the torch that helps to enlighten the young. They take part in the expectations as observed in the African proverb: "It takes a village to raise a child." In time, they come to old age and qualify to be addressed as elders, among whom are found the sages and seers of the community.

Death

Death is the time when the soul leaves the body to become a spirit. African mythology allots a great deal of space to the subject of death. Usually the same myths of creation that trace the origin of human beings include the origin of death. In these myths, death often comes to the world because of human misdeeds. Although African people accept death as a natural part of the life cycle, they generally feel that each individual death always has a cause associated with supernatural powers. These include mystical powers like magic, witchcraft, and sorcery.

The understanding of death brings with it the realization that a person's body and soul are no longer one. In dying, the individual has joined the world of the departed. This fact usually evokes sorrow for those left behind. A spiritual period of mourning sets in, with funeral rites that vary by ethnic group.

Death calls for a ritual disposal of the body of the deceased. Burial rites are performed by the community. Those attending the burial bid farewell to the deceased by throwing a bit of soil or flower petals into the grave before the burial is completed. People are very attentive to giving the departed a proper funeral. It is important that the spirit of the departed be contented in the world beyond and not come back as a dissatisfied ghost to plague those left behind.

Final Funeral Rites

In many African traditions there are final funeral rites. These mark the end of the time of mourning. At this time the designated heir of the deceased is officially declared, installed, and invested with the ritual instruments that entitle him or her to the inheritance. Connected to the final funeral rites is the idea that the deceased may be reincarnated, or reborn, into a newborn life through naming. During this time, the deceased becomes increasingly identified with the world of the spirits among whom he or she now dwells.

Ritual

Rituals are religiously meaningful acts that people perform in appropriate circumstances, usually following strictly prescribed patterns. Rituals are the concrete expression of belief. African believers, and indeed, believers of all religions, feel that they have to show their belief in some way. They do this by worshiping the Supreme Being, by doing reverence to superhuman beings, and by paying due respect to their fellow humans. Prayer, music, and dancing enhance the effectiveness of ritual acts. Sacrifices and offerings help to confirm the relationship between the Supreme Being, superhumanity, and humanity. Rituals take place during community celebrations and festivals for the purpose of thanksgiving, purification, and communion. Their performance helps to link humanity with superhumanity.

Prayer

In African religion there are countless prayers. Like other African religious literature, they are handed down orally from generation to generation. Many prayers are traditional and centuries old. Most are recited by people in official capacities. These include priests and priestesses, diviners, rainmakers, medicinemen and women, kings, chiefs, ritual and family elders, and heads of organized groups, such as hunters. Prayers are usually addressed to God, superhuman beings, and ancestors.

People in search of spiritual assistance for a variety of human needs address their prayers to the powers above. People pray for life, health, healing, wealth, and prosperity. They pray for success at work. They pray to be delivered from difficulties. They address prayers either directly or indirectly through intermediaries for all spiritual assistance possible. They pray in praise, they pray in joy, and they pray in thanksgiving.

Before a couple marry, their families negotiate the traditional bride pay-ment, or lobola. *People believe that the groom respects the bride more if he must pay for her. Traditionally the lobola was paid in cows, but now it is usually paid in cash. After the groom pays the lobola, there are other ceremonies in which gifts are exchanged. At the end, the groom receives a sheep or a goat. This gift shows that the bride's fami-ly has accepted him.*

Early on the wedding morning, the groom's family slaughters a cow, which is cooked and eaten for the wedding feast. The bride's family watches, making sure that the meat is divided equally between the two families. They sing and exchange gifts. In the afternoon, the bride arrives. She wears the traditional Zulu costume with a leopard skin neckpiece and a beaded hat and skirt. With her family carrying her hope chest, she tours the groom's property. This symbolically intro-duces her to the groom's family.

The families gather in a wide circle. The men, wearing Zulu costume, dance. Then there is an exchange of presents from the bride to mem-bers of the groom's family. These are usually blankets and mats. The recipients dance or sing their thanks. The groom's gift, a blanket, comes last. It is presented to him in a skit, where it is thrown over his head. The bride's friends beat him playfully, indicating what they will do if he does not treat the bride well, until he escapes. With the exchange of gifts over, the feast begins. The feast seals the marriage. When the two families have eaten together, the couple is joined as one.

Music

Music is an audible expression of African prayer. There are many religious songs in praise of God and superhuman beings. There are many songs intended to express joy for spiritual bless-ings. There are songs asking favors from above. And there are songs exuberantly sung in thanksgiving. Songs are usually accompanied by the beating of drums and the playing of other instruments.

Dance

Whereas song is religious expression in voice, dancing con-centrates on expressing religious emotions, elegance, and

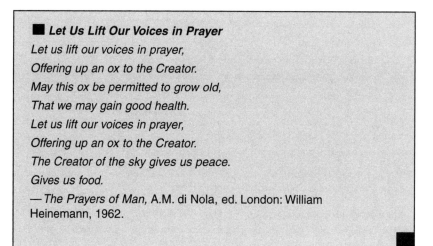

■ Let Us Lift Our Voices in Prayer

Let us lift our voices in prayer,
Offering up an ox to the Creator.
May this ox be permitted to grow old,
That we may gain good health.
Let us lift our voices in prayer,
Offering up an ox to the Creator.
The Creator of the sky gives us peace.
Gives us food.
—*The Prayers of Man,* A.M. di Nola, ed. London: William Heinemann, 1962.

dynamism through bodily movement. African religious ritual would be lifeless without the accompaniment of music and dancing. These are powerful means of African religious expression.

Sacrifice

Sacrifice is giving up something valuable in order to render homage to some superior being. A sacrifice is thus a gift offered to God or to a superhuman being in recognition of their superiority over humanity. Of all acts of worship to the Supreme Being, sacrifices and offerings are emphasized most. The Abaluyia of Kenya refer to God as "the One to whom sacred rites and sacrifices are made." Animal sacrifice is the usual way of offering praise. Bulls, goats, or chickens are the most common objects of sacrifice, offered at every stage of the rites of passage.

Communal Ritual

Prayer, music, songs, drums, other musical instruments, dancing, and sacrifice come together in vividly orchestrated communal ritual. These rituals celebrate such things as purification rites, communion rites, and agricultural rites.

Agricultural rites have to do with the way people use land for the production of food. Farming is one of the most important preoccupations of the people. Its importance requires the blessings of God and those of the superhuman guardians of the people. For that reason, each stage of agricultural development calls for spiritual assistance. Primary is the need for rain. Rain is so important that there are special rites, and indeed, ritual specialists whose main function is to bring about rain at crucial times.

There are rites concerned with the preparation of new fields. There are planting rites and harvest rites. At the time of sowing and harvesting, African religious traditions have important communal ceremonies that link the people's agricultural activities with the spirits of the community. In preparation of the field a farmer in Ghana brings offerings of a fowl and cooked yam for the spirit of the earth and for his ancestors. As the blood of the fowl drips on the earth and the yam he says, "Grandfather (mentions the name) you once came and hoed here and then you left it to me. You also, Earth, Ya, on whose soil I am going to hoe, the yearly cycle has come round and I am going to cultivate; when I work, let a fruitful year come upon me, do not let a knife cut me, do not let a tree break and fall upon me, do not let a snake bite me."

When the land is tilled and planted, people of all African cultures ask blessings from the superhuman beings. At the time of ripening and harvest, they hold "first fruits" ceremonies. According to tradition, superhuman powers must eat of the first fruits of harvest before human beings partake of them. They must receive their share in offering before anything is given to anyone else. To deprive them of their important place in the hierarchy would induce them to take revenge by threatening the future harvest. The first fruits ceremonies are festival times for offering thanksgiving to the superhuman powers for the new harvest.

Ritual Leaders

Ritual leaders are those members of the community who preside over and conduct a particular religious ritual. They come to their leadership roles in different ways. Some positions are hereditary. Others are the result of a special spiritual calling,

A portrait of Ssekabaka Muteesa II. In the language of the Baganda people of the kingdom of Buganda in Uganda, ssekabaka means "late king." The reigning king is known as kabaka. In his capacity as king, the kabaka is the supreme head of Baganda religion.

along with special training. This category of African ritual leaders includes rulers, priests, mediums, diviners, healers, rainmakers, elders, and sages.

African Rulers

African people consider the authority of their leaders to come from God. Their rulers are political leaders, but they are also true religious leaders. In African traditions there is no such thing as "separation of church and state." Religion and human affairs, such as politics, by African religious standards, go hand in hand.

Kings, queens, or chiefs have both privileges and duties. Their position carries with it outstanding power, authority, and influence. But although rulers are endowed with power and prerogative, they are also bound by obligations and kept in check by taboos. The ruler is the father/mother of the people and the symbol of their ethnic unity. He or she must therefore solve human problems and give an ear to all subjects, as well as representing the people in contact with other powers.

In many countries the king is the high priest of the people. As high priest, he is not only in charge of matters of government, but also of religious matters. For example, in Buganda, part of Uganda in East Africa, the veneration of the national gods is under the immediate control of the *kabaka*, or king. By his authority, temples are built to the different gods. He has the ultimate power to confirm or reject the choice of priests made by the clans according to the traditions surrounding the different gods.

Besides being the primary religious leader of the people, the ruler is closely connected with ritual traditions. Ritual occasions connected with kingship or chiefdom, such as coronation, enthronement, and funeral rites, connect strongly to the sacredness of the ruler. Rulers are regarded as God's earthly representatives. They are the reflection of God's rule in the universe. To many African peoples, rulers are not ordinary men or women. They are living symbols of the connection between the Supreme Being, the superhuman beings, and the human beings.

Priests

In African religious tradition, a priest is a ritual leader who oversees, administers, and coordinates religious matters for the community. Priests may be men or women. Priests are key figures in maintaining the religious affairs of an African ethnic group. Priests are usually attached to a temple of a god and are charged with its care. People become priests by both vocation and training. However, there are a few African societies like the Baamba, the Banyankore, and the Basoga of Uganda, the Bavenda of South Africa, the Binawa and the Srubu of Nigeria, and the Sonjo of Tanzania in which priesthood is hereditary.

People believe that priests and priestesses are called by God. Some are said to have been set aside from birth. Others are said to have been called by a god through being possessed by his or her spirit. At other times parents send a child to be trained as a priest because the child was born in answer to prayer, and so is dedicated to the service of God. Trainees are submitted to the guidance of an older priest. Training is usually arduous. It may last some years, during which the child learns the secrets of serving a god.

Mediums

Mediums are people who can contact the spirit world, usually by being possessed by spirits. As a rule, they become mediums through being possessed by superhuman beings, after which they undergo training. Mediums are usually women. They are attached either to a priest at a temple or to a diviner. They sink into a trance, usually induced by music, drumming, and singing, and become possessed. The spirit speaks through the medium, transmitting messages from the spirit world to human beings. Sometimes the message may be in a strange language, and the priest or an assistant may be called to interpret.

Diviners

Diviners are ritual leaders whose special position is to unveil the mysteries of the past and future. In so doing, they pronounce what may be causing problems in the community. Diviners not only read the signs of the present, but they also have techniques by which they discover hidden knowledge about the past, the present, and the future of those who consult them. To find out the unknown for a client, diviners may use shells, pebbles, water, animal entrails, and many other objects regarded as "mirrors." From these, they read why something has gone wrong.

In some African traditions the work of diviners is so revered that they are elevated to the position of divinities. For instance, in the Yoruba religion the diviner is known as the Father of Mysteries, with a spiritual patronage of no less than *Orunmila,* the Yoruba deity of divination.

People usually become diviners either by training or by inheritance. Diviners-to-be are privately trained by experienced diviners. In many cases the training period may last from three to seven years. They must master the oral tradition, which

■ *An Ashanti stool, or kontonkorowi. This circular rainbow stool is used by the kings and chiefs of the Ashanti of Ghana in West Africa. In Ashanti religion, such stools are associated with a leader's soul and highly esteemed.*

involves memorizing names and signs of divination as well as figures, proverbs, and stories connected with them. They learn to use the instruments of divination, such as pebbles, seeds, gourds, numbers, cowrie shells, and so forth. They also learn how to read animal entrails, to read palms, to form images or use images in pots of water, and to interpret sounds.

Healer

In some parts of Africa, a healer is called *musawo,* "a person with a bag." Healers are easily distinguished by the bag they carry and by their attire. Healers customarily wear amulets, shells, and other decorative accessories that ordinary people do not wear. The bag that they carry is their trademark. In it are all types of medicines.

In a broad sense, healers are ritual leaders whose service relies on supernatural powers. They come to the aid of the community in matters of health and well-being. Healers work in conjunction with other ritual leaders to keep the members of the community physically and spiritually healthy.

Healers are variously referred to as *medicine men* or *women, herbalists,* and sometimes as *witch doctors.* They are some of the most influential people in an African community. Their influence comes from their important work of curing members of the community of illness and disease. Their gifts are both material and spiritual. Materially, they have wide knowledge of healing herbs and medications. Spiritually, they heal the underlying spiritual causes of illness.

In African thought, illness is always caused by superhuman agencies or by extrahuman forces such as magic, witchcraft, and sorcery. Therefore someone who is sick must determine the spiritual cause of an illness in order to cure it. Answers to the question of why an illness has occurred may come from the spirit world in oracles or divine pronouncements through the cooperation of a priest and a medium. Or they may come from the superhuman and extrahuman world through the cooperation of a diviner. Oracles and divination are the means of identifying the cause of illness and the illness itself. When the illness is identified, the healer can devise the cure. Healers then turn to the spirit world for help in getting and administering the right medicine.

Healers are often specialists. Some focus on performing healing rituals in combination with other ritual leaders. Others may concentrate on one aspect of healing, such as bonesetting, herbal remedies, or dietary prescriptions. Their specialties depend on how the healer received his or her calling. Some healers are healers by inheritance. Their craft is handed down from parents or relatives. Others learn the trade from experienced healers with whom they study and work for a substantial length of time before they are allowed to practice on their own.

Rainmakers

Rain, so essential to agriculture and therefore to survival, is closely connected to African religion. The Dinka of Sudan know the Supreme Being as Deng or Dengdit, which literally means "rain." The Gikuyu of Kenya know God as Ngai. Ngai has three capacities. By the first he sends rain and riches, by the second he sends good wives and healthy children, by the third, sickness and loss. It is in the first capacity that Ngai is considered to be the Supreme Being and is credited with divine powers. The Churi and Masai of Eastern Africa and the Ewe of Western Africa say of rain, "God is falling" or "God is weeping." Other African people say "God's blessings are falling." They view rain as divine influence that descends to earth. The continued fertility of the land requires rain. When it fails to fall, people begin to wonder what they may have done wrong. They feel a need to set right whatever has caused a problem between them and the Supreme Being or the spirit world. They call for the ritual leadership that comes from those known as rainmakers.

Rainmakers are specialists in religious matters pertaining to rain. They determine the reasons why rain fails to fall or why there is too much rain. Rainmakers perform rites of prayer or sacrifices offered to ensure that enough rain will fall at the proper times. They also preside over prayers and sacrifices offered to check excessive rainfall. They are thus both rainmakers and rain-stoppers.

The Asantehene, or king of the Ashanti people, stands under the symbolic umbrella of his authority in the company of his subjects. As king, he is the supreme head of the Ashanti religion.

A person may become a rainmaker either by training or by inheritance. Through messages from the spirit world and through dreams, a person may find a call to become a rainmaker. Then that person may train under an experienced rainmaker. Quite a long period of training is required before the person can enter a serious practice. There are also rainmakers who achieve this religious and ritual position by inheritance. Most renowned of these is the Queen of the Balovedu of Southern Africa, who is called a "rain-queen." She is not primarily a ruler, but a rainmaker. People rely on her for their security not in regard to regimentation, armies, and organization, but on her power to make rain for them and to withhold rain from their enemies.

Rituals in African Life

Whether they are passing through the regular stages of the life cycle, observing the agricultural cycle, consulting a medium, a healer, or a rainmaker, African people are in regular contact with the sacred in their daily lives. They are aware at all times of their debt to the Supreme Being and of their reliance on the local gods for their food, their health, their prosperity, and their well-being. The traditional rituals of African religions reinforce their reliance on the superhuman powers that surround them.

CHAPTER 6

Sacred Spaces
and Places

The places where the rites and rituals of African religion are carried out are African *sacred space*. Some of these places are constructed specifically for religious purposes, but others are natural places in the environment where people come together for ritual purposes. There are also places that would normally be regarded as nonsacred but which may on occasion serve as ritual spaces. These are often homes in which senior family members may officiate as ritual elders.

Sacred Space

Some places are made sacred through the relics of divine beings. For example, the Uganda Museum in Uganda is only a museum to the general visitor. But since British colonial times, relics of the local gods have been confined there. For local people, this building is therefore a sacred space. When they visit the museum, they do so with care and with a sense of awe and mystery. So a museum visit becomes a casual sort of ritual.

The gods may also signal the special sanctity of a place in some way. Animals, by their symbolic relationships to the gods as well as by their ritual guardianship of a locality, often are

signs of communication from the spirit world. Their appearance in a certain locality may mark that place as sacred.

In a larger sense, people understand the whole land of their particular culture and ethnic group to be sacred. The narratives of the sacred origins of the land and its people communicate this sacredness. For this reason, present-day political leaders who ignore the sacredness of a people's lands often become the cause of unrest.

Viewing the Universe: The Zulu

According to the Zulu of South Africa, the Zulu people were not specifically created, but originated in heaven. In their language, *zulu* means sky and/or heaven. *Zulu* also means the Zulu people or the Zulu ethnic group. *iNkosi yeZulu* means the "Lord of the Sky/Heaven" in whom the Zulu originate. In other words the very being of anything pertaining to the Zulu is regarded as originating in heaven, or *ezulwini,* which might be translated as the "above." From there the process of origination continues down to earth and below the surface of the earth in the region of the universe called *phansi,* which means "the habitation place of spirits."

Spiritual Geography

Africans have long associated the wonders of nature with religion. In African tradition, anything that seems to be shrouded in mystery has tended to evoke a sense of the religious, and the natural world is filled with beauty and mystery.

For African people, the whole universe is filled with religious spirit. In African religion, all elements of the universe are regarded as symbols of the divine. The sacred space of the universe has three parts. Above the earth is the sky, or heaven, the home of the Supreme Being. Below the earth is the realm of the spirits, which keeps humanity connected to the land. In the middle is the earth, the world of humanity and the here and now.

The Sky

The African sky inspires much religious feeling. High in the heavens, the blazing Sun and glowing Moon inspire humanity

■ *An akuba figurine. This is the Ashanti figure of fertility carved in wood statuettes worn by girls and women to assure childbearing.*

with awe. The night sky is embellished with thousands upon thousands of twinkling stars that, on a clear night, can leave observers in a state of wonder.

Sun, Moon, and Earth all carry aspects of divinity. Among African peoples in all corners of the African continent, the Sun is a symbol of the Supreme Being. In that sense, God as the Supreme Being is called Kazooba, meaning the power that is as high and as powerful as the Sun. In general, the Moon is recognized as being a natural phenomenon that carries sacredness, serenity, and tenderness. For that reason Africans mark the appearance of the new Moon with rituals that express the sacredness of the Moon.

In many African traditions the idea of the Supreme Being combines both masculine and feminine. The Sun represents the masculine element in God, while the Moon represents the feminine. But in some African societies, these gender roles change, so the Moon is masculine. In any case, positioned in between the Sun and the Moon, the earth has the symbolic role of mother to humanity.

The Natural World

The earth, too, is a source of wonder. Africa's geography is extremely varied.

Natural landmarks include mountains, oceans, lakes, rivers, waterfalls, forests, rocks, caves, and trees, any or all of which may inspire religious feelings. The forest and plains are alive with a great variety of animals, chattering birds, creeping reptiles, spiders and insects, all of which, by inhabiting the world with humans, beg the question of their place in the universe.

Although almost any geographical feature may become the focus of worship, mountains and hills are the features usually identified as being sacred. The people who live near the great African mountains, such as Mt. Kilimanjaro, Mt. Kenya, Mt. Rwenzori or the Mountains of the Moon, Mt. Elgon, and Mt. Cameroon, make sacrifices and offerings, perform rituals, and offer prayers to the Supreme Being and other spiritual powers on or beside such places. Other natural sites such as trees, islands, lakes, rivers, and waterfalls may also be designated as sacred spaces.

Ritual Places and Objects

For Africans, ritual places are human-made structures or marked areas at which religious rites may be observed. These include shrines, tombs, temples, and sacred localities. Since the beginning of time, Africans have sensed a great invisible power, a vital force, which surrounds and is part of all nature. To help themselves come to terms with this power, Africans have devised ways of containing it by inviting it to reside in human-made places and objects, so that they may perceive it in smaller doses.

Places built for religious purposes may be temples and other constructed shrines. Temples are architectural structures that vary in size and shape. Other constructed shrines may vary from a pillar or monument to a small stone or an iron or wooden marker. Examples of such shrines include the Staff of Oranyan and the Central Shrine of the powerful Ogun in Ile Ife.

Temples

A temple is a place or a building where people congregate to worship, to pray, and to ask for favors from spiritual powers. There are numerous types of temples in Africa, constructed according to the various traditions of different peoples. There are large temples, small ones, and even miniature ones. Many have been overwhelmed by the appearance in Africa of religions like Christianity and Islam, but others have persisted and have been adapted to contemporary colonial types of architecture. One of the most conspicuous temple buildings in Africa south of the Sahara is connected with Great Zimbabwe. This is a stone building of complex construction devoted to the worship of Mwari, the Shona name of the Supreme Being, and cults of the *mhondoro*, the spirits associated with the ruling dynasties in this Southern African area.

Temples in other parts of Africa, built by the people and attended by priests and priestesses, often follow the pattern of local construction. In the Kingdom of Buganda in Uganda, these may be conical and thatched. Some Nigerian temples, like the Obatala and the Ifa temples of Ife, represent African religious temples built on the basis of Western architectural influence.

Shrines

In African religion, a shrine is any container, box, or receptacle that may receive and contain superhuman power. A shrine is therefore an anchorage, or place of rest, for spiritual powers. As a constructed structure, in addition to natural landmarks, a shrine marks the sacred geography of a religious tradition.

Tombs

The tradition of tomb-building in Africa goes back to centuries-old tombs like the pyramids of ancient Egypt and Nubia. Helping us to trace back some vital religious ideas, pyramids express belief in divinity as well as in the immortality of the soul. There are many other representative types of religiously expressive tombs, among which is the Kasubi tomb of the Kabakas of Buganda in Uganda. These tombs are tended by young priestesses, who keep the fires within them and perform rites that worshipers may attend. The tombs thus serve as places where ordinary people may be in touch with the higher powers.

Marked Localities of Religious Significance

In many African religious traditions there are localities that are identified as shrines without the construction of elaborate buildings or structures. For example, the shrine of Ogun, a Yoruba divinity considered to be one of the most powerful as the chief blacksmith in heaven and a bloodthirsty hunter on earth, is

■ Chi wara *is an antelope-like mask used by the Bambara people of Mali in West Africa in rites aimed at helping produce abundant agricultural products.*

a locality in Ife marked by stumps of wood and by stones. It is at such a shrine that his followers, who include hunters, blacksmiths, engineers, mechanics, drivers, artisans, and all people who deal in iron, steel, or other metals, go to seek spiritual help.

Ritual Objects

Ritual objects, such as talismans or statues, are used in observing African religious rites. The use of ritual places and objects goes far back in African tradition. Ritual objects are comparatively small human-made items. One such item is a shrine-object, a small amulet or charm that is believed to carry spiritual power. These objects may be produced in a multitude of forms. They may be owned communally or personally. Other religious objects are usually works of art with religious themes, such as masks or statues of gods. They may also be items intended for utilitarian purposes, like pitchers or pots, which because of religious decoration or form may spontaneously be considered religious objects.

Sacred Space in African Life

At home, in temples and shrines, and in the countryside, African people are aware of the sacredness around them. Although they may congregate in a particular place or turn toward a particular geographical feature during prayer, they have a continuing sense that superhuman beings walk beside them in their daily lives. Their presence makes all places potentially sacred. Sacredness may be more concentrated in a place built or designated as sacred, but in fact it is everywhere. The objects that African people create and place on shrines and in their homes are continuing reminders of this sacredness.

CHAPTER 7

Mystical Forces

African people feel the power and energy of the spirit world that is all around them. They experience the actions of gods and ancestors in everything they do. African people are deeply aware of the powerful force of creation that put them on the earth and guides their footsteps. They are closely attuned to the mystical and mysterious superhuman powers in their lives.

In addition to their sense of the vital force of the universe, Africans recognize other types of forces that are neither superhuman nor simply human but lie somewhere between. These mystical forces include magic, witchcraft, and sorcery. Like spiritual forces, they affect people's lives and the lives of their community.

Magic, Witchcraft, and Sorcery

Magic

Magic is the practice of manipulating mysterious forces for practical purposes. People who are able to bring about magic are known as magicians. In African belief, magic is a far cry from the smoke and mirrors of the Western theater stage. African magic does not have to do with illusion or trickery. It is a true religious

element. Africans believe that magic is neutral. It may be used for good ends as it may also be used for evil ones.

Magic and religion are so closely related as to be almost one. The Ewe of Ghana believe that God sent magic power into the world after he had created the first person. The Langi of Uganda add that the art of magic originated partly in God and partly in the spirits. However, they are not certain as to when this took place. The Azande of Sudan note that the art of magic, together with the knowledge of making medicines and the ability to avenge crimes, were given to humanity by God. The Bemba of Central Africa simply put it that magic is a gift from God. Behind these beliefs about magic is the general belief that God is the creator of everything, including this puzzling force of magic.

African religion is mainly concerned with asking the cooperation of the Supreme Being and superhuman beings for the well-being of humanity. In the sense that ritual leaders are able to call upon the higher powers effectively, there is always something of a magician in the personality of a ritual leader.

Magic in African religion, as it is also in many other religions, makes the unknown less threatening and provides psychological reassurances for potentially difficult or even dangerous situations. Although Westerners do not call it magic, there are many magical things people do, often without knowing they are doing them, that an African would consider to be magic at work. It is magic when a baseball player crosses himself before stepping up to the plate in order to get a hit. It is for magical protection that a truck driver places a rosary on the dashboard. Ritual acts and talismans provide magical protection from unknown dangers around the world.

Witchcraft

Traditionally, African people believe that witchcraft is one of the causes of misfortunes in a community. Witchcraft is a dreaded element in African society. People define witchcraft as the state of being possessed by extrahuman forces that can do evil or harm. A sizable population of Africans at all levels of society believe in witchcraft. They hold witchcraft responsible for

■ *A South African healer seeks to find the cause of an illness through the use of mystical forces.*

■ *An indigenous magician, in working attire.*

such misfortunes as failure to bear children, diseases, failure in life, illness, and death.

People understand witchcraft to be part of the religious forces that surround them. The Nupe of Nigeria say that, in the context of creation, "God also put the power of witchcraft in the world." The Barundi of Burundi add, "God gives power to the magicians and witches." But although witchcraft may be a creation of God, he also protects against it. The Igbo of Nigeria assert that "God punishes those who do evil and protects people against witchcraft." The Nyakyusa of Tanzania note that "God has the power to drive away witches." Witches are men or women who have within themselves the power to practice witchcraft.

Witchcraft and magic are related, but they are distinct from each other. The Azande people, for example, make a firm distinction between magic, *ngwa,* and witchcraft, *mangu. Mangu* is hereditary. It can be traced to a substance that can be found by autopsy in the stomach of a witch. It exerts a sinister influence over the lives of others in the community when it is roused by bad intentions. *Ngwa* is not identified with any special substance. It is divided into good magic and bad magic.

People have a variety of views about how someone becomes a witch. They most commonly believe that the trait is inherited from a parent. In that sense, some people are born

---

■ *Magic*

In magic, certain gestures, words, or acts, separately or together, are believed to invoke the direct assistance of supernatural powers in human affairs or to give people control over the secret powers of Nature. In another sense, magic may be defined as the art of living in intimate union with Nature and sharing and using its secrets through ritual or "doing."

The profession of magician is held in esteem. It is passed on from father to son. As priest the magician promoted the welfare of the community; as medicine man he healed the ailing.

from *African Sculpture Speaks,* by Ladislas Segy. New York: Hill and Wang, 1969, p. 12.

witches. In the case of hereditary witchcraft, it is possible for someone to be a witch and not know it, although eventually the witch notices his or her powers. These powers can be used to cast a spell and do harm to someone. Not all witchcraft is hereditary, however. People also feel that witchcraft can be "caught" like an infection, or that someone who wants to be a witch can buy the power from another witch.

Witchcraft causes evil and unrest in a community. The community fights its influence by calling on healers who specialize in curing the effects of witchcraft. These healers have come to be known as "witch-doctors," a term that is often misunderstood. Witch doctors are not witches themselves. That is, they are not evil people who want to harm their neighbors. They are respected members of society whose function is not to harm but to heal. A witch doctor helps those who believe they have been bewitched.

The possibility of witchcraft is everywhere. People seek protection against it in a variety of ways. On the personal level, they may use amulets, charms, or talismans to help ward off the presence of evil. A hunter, for example, may wear a piece of a tooth of a lion as protection against witchcraft during a hunting expedition. A pregnant woman may wear a talisman around her waist to protect her unborn child against witchcraft. The head of a household may hang an amulet on the doorpost of his house for protection of those within.

People may also seek protection from witchcraft for their community through prayer. Following are some prayers against witchcraft.

Be Good to Us

I offer thee this dege, *this* d'lo *[nut], and this chicken*
in the sacrifice that I carry out in my name and in the
*   name of my children.*
Keep us safe from the suba *[witches], from all evil and*
*   ugly spirits.*
Be good to us, keep us from sickness, give us women,
*   healthy children*
and take care to send us rain; give us physical vigor
and in all ways preserve us that we may gather a
*   bountiful crop.*

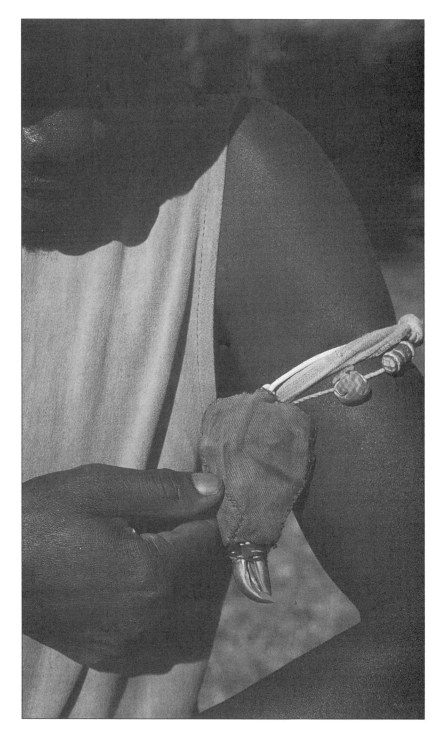

■ An amulet or charm
worn by a person from
Senegal, West Africa, to
help ward off evil spirits.

■ *On the stool are cloths and cowrie shells, relics of Kibuuka, the god of national defense for the Baganda of Uganda.*

If It Be a Witch

Repeat my words ee!
You Flesh of my father, I call you in my prayer,
because of a man who came to bewitch and left his
    fishing spear behind.
Therefore I call you to hear me.
A man became sick because of a witch
And I have thought thus:
if it be a child who brought the spear and forgot it, then
    I have no quarrel with him.
But if it be a witch who came to bewitch,
then you Flesh of my father show him your strength,
that he may see for himself what you can do.
I have no long speech to make to you, I shall soon
    be silent.

Sorcery

The *Oxford English Dictionary* traces the word *sorcery* to 1330 B.C.E. It means the "use of magic or enchantment; the practice of magic arts; witchcraft." To Africans, however, the "magic arts" are nothing artistic or enchanting. The African understanding of sorcery is as something darker and more dangerous. It is the use of magic to do harm. Sorcery shares this quality with witchcraft. The difference is in degree. Witchcraft may be defined as a mystical and innate power, which can be used by its possessor to harm other people, whereas sorcery is evil magic against others.

Sorcerers set out to do harm. Unlike witches, who may cast spells or call on mystical forces to do their mischief, sorcerers resort to artificial means, such as poison, to ply their craft. For example, they grow long fingernails in which to hide the harmful potions that they may drop in someone's food or drink. In African understanding, sorcerers are frankly evil. They cause much trouble in a community in the form of discontent, illness, and even death. Some African societies specifically refer to sorcerers or sorceresses as "poisoners." Theirs is evil magic, deliberately aimed at harming people and communities. As in the case of witchcraft, people turn to healers for defenses against sorcery.

Mystical Forces in African Life

To African believers, there is nothing imaginary about extrahuman forces. People believe deeply in the influence of these forces on their lives. Extrahuman forces are not to be taken lightly. The following event, reported as fact, illustrates just how powerful these forces, and the belief in them, can be.

During the early 1960s, an incident occurred through a combination of influences of superhuman and extrahuman powers. A husband and wife were quarreling. The situation deteriorated to the point that the husband consulted a medicine man. This medicine man, whose name was Kigangali, lived in a village called Mushanga, in the district of Ankore in Uganda. No ordinary medicine man, Kigangali was known for his remarkable command of mystical forces. Kigangali told the husband of Nzeera, the quarrelsome wife, that he would take care of the situation. Exactly what Kigangali did is unknown, but the effect of his magical manipulations was that Nzeera was turned into a lion.

Perhaps in the hope that she could be turned back into a woman through exorcism, people captured the lion and dragged it to the Christian parish center in Mushanga. Observers came from all over the area to witness what had happened. Before anything could be done, however, the lion died, and the woman's soul with it. The lion was buried with the rites due a human being; the woman was never seen again.

Almost 40 years later, this extraordinary event is still discussed because of the sense of awe and wonder it created. To call down such powerful mystical forces is both terrible and wonderful, repellent and attractive. Yet those who believe in them have no doubt that such powers are real, and the changing of a woman into a lion is clear proof.

CHAPTER **8**

African Religion in Today's World

*I*n the last half of the 20th century, African religion has finally achieved its rightful place on the world's stage. The technological revolution that created radio, television, telephone, faxes, and e-mail has shrunk the world to a global village. In the early 1900s, it took nine months to travel from the United States to the interior of Africa. Today it takes about 12 hours by air to reach Entebbe, Uganda, the most centrally positioned international airport in the heart of Africa. Technology and air travel have made Africa a close neighbor to the rest of the world.

Becoming a World Religion

Over history, people from outside the African continent have tended to misunderstand and to dismiss African religion, often because of stereotyping and prejudice. One clear indication of this is that until quite recently, African religions were not considered "true" religions, not included on the list of world religions. Only lately has African religion received serious recognition as a world religion.

In the most important sense, of course, African religion has always been a world religion, but historically it has not been

recognized as one. The followers of Islam who established their influence on Africa's east coast in the 10th century called Africans *kaffirs,* or unbelievers. In the 15th century, when the Christians arrived, they accepted the term, and even went so far as to call the entire region Kaffraria. The idea that Africans were a people with no religion was widely accepted. African religious practices became known as *fetishism*—superstition and magic.

It took 300 years for scholars to recognize African religion as a true religion. At first, they called African beliefs and practices "primitive religion." This term recognized African beliefs as valid, yet "primitive" suggests something crude and unformed, whereas African religious practices were often highly refined. Eventually the religions of Africa came to be known simply as "African religion."

In 1957, Ghana in West Africa shook off the shackles of colonialism and became independent. This began a general movement toward independence in Africa. Political independence meant a return to African roots and a new appreciation of things African. It restored the "Africanness" of the African people. One outcome was that African religion experienced a comeback. By this time, too, the Western world had come to a greater appreciation and understanding of the value of African religion. In the 1964 Vatican II Council, Roman Catholic bishops from all over the world met in Rome. They accepted African religion as a full partner among world religions. The influence of Vatican II spread well beyond the Catholic Church. Observers from almost all Christian denominations attended and carried its message back to their churches. They, too, quickly moved to accept African religion in its many manifestations as a full partner among world religions. With this official recognition and an objective approach to study, African religion is now recognized as among the world's great religions.

Ubuntu

African religion is deeply and fundamentally humanistic, centered on the human condition. This humanism colors all of life and its relationships. African humanism may be summarized in the principle of *Ubuntu. Ubuntu* is difficult to translate, but as

South Africa's Archbishop Desmond Tutu, the Nobel Prize–winning churchman, has said, "You know when it is there, and it is obvious when it is absent. It has to do with what it means to be truly human, it refers to gentleness, to compassion, to hospitality, to openness to others, to vulnerability, to be available for others and to know that you are bound up with them in the bundle of life, for a person is only a person through other persons." This is the principle behind African religion. Ultimately, this is the principle that empowers African religion to exert worldwide influence.

■ *Archbishop Desmond Mpilo Tutu, the Nobel Peace Prize winner whose concern for humanity is deeply grounded in the African idea of* Ubuntu.

Influence on Religion Worldwide

African religion has great influence on African society and on African people throughout the world. All people of African heritage are tied to African religion by the bonds of culture.

Their environment shapes their religious feelings and ideas. Although they may convert to other religions, people cannot give up their Africanness. It is too much a part of them. And a part of that Africanness is African religion. Even if they are Christians or Muslims, as many Africans are, they have formed their feelings about religion in general on the basis of their African roots. They appreciate African religion as a religion in its own right. They are conscious of both its unity and its great diversity. But it also affects people from outside the African continent who are indebted to it in ways they may not recognize.

The influence of African religion creeps into the realms of other religions. Many Christians in Africa today are what are called "daylight Christians." These are people who profess Christianity but who simultaneously practice African religion. As an example, they may seek medical help through a Christian-administered medical clinic but also decide to consult a traditional healer.

The influence of African religion goes beyond the African continent. There is no part of the world today that does not feel the African presence. In the Western Hemisphere, for example, elements of African religion appear in a number of local religious traditions. In Brazil, Candomblé and Macumba are two religions whose backbone is African. In the Caribbean, religions with strong African roots include Haitian Voodoo, which is based on the Fon Vodun worship; Cuban Santería, a blend of African and Christian beliefs; Trinidadian Shango; and Jamaican Rastafarianism. Emigration has carried all of these to the United States. In addition, traditions like the African Methodist Episcopal Church, which traces its beginnings to the time of slavery, incorporate elements of African religion.

Within Africa, people have adapted Christian beliefs and rituals to fit their own needs, establishing churches of their own. Many of these churches have strong elements of African religion. People felt that Christianity, with its emphasis on salvation in the next world, was not meeting their needs for the here and now. It did not, for example, offer protection against witches, ways of divining the future, and healing, which the new churches offer. The Aldura Church of Yoruba features leaders who act as healers and diviners. By some estimates, more than 7,000,000 Africans belong to the new churches. Another factor in their development has been people's need to shake off outside influences and take local control of their religion.

Kwanzaa

Kwanzaa is an African-American holiday. It was begun in 1966 by Maulana Karenga. This holiday pays tribute to the rich cultural roots of African Americans. *Kwanzaa* is an African word meaning "the first fruits of the harvest," and the holiday is based on African first fruits celebrations. These are yearly celebrations with a fourfold purpose: to bring people together; to honor and pay reverence to the Creator and Creation; to commemorate the past; and to give the people the opportunity to recommit themselves to the highest ideals of the community. These ideals are summarized in the seven principles of unity, self-determination, collective work and responsibility, cooperative economics, purpose, creativity, and faith.

Kwanzaa is celebrated annually from December 26 through January 1. The ritual instruments of Kwanzaa include a straw placemat, a seven branched candleholder, seven candles, a variety of fruits, ears of corn, a symbolic representation of the number of children in the home by ears of corn, a communal cup that represents unity, and a drink that is poured and shared together.

Kwanzaa is usually presented as a unique holiday—neither religious, political, nor heroic, but cultural. However, as with all things African, it is impossible to separate religion from culture, and Kwanzaa carries religious associations along with cultural ones.

African Music

Music, either vocal or instrumental, usually accompanies African religious ritual. Music is used to praise the Supreme Being, the superhuman beings, and the ancestors. It is used as prayer in supplication for favors from heaven. The drum is the primary instrument. It is a key to unlock communication with the spirit world. People beat or play drums to induce oracles from high above, through mediums.

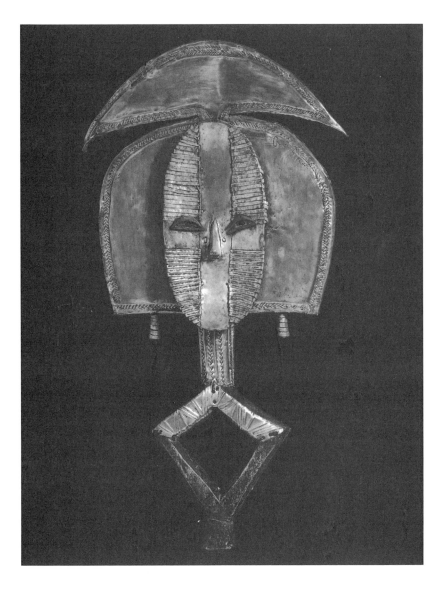

A mbulu-ngulu, or reliquary, used in rites to ward off evil spirits by the Bakota people of the Republic of Congo, in Central Africa. In 1907, Pablo Picasso painted a variety of renditions using this design.

African Americans originated one of America's earliest original musical forms, the Negro spiritual. Negro spirituals, now familiar worldwide, were the creation of African Americans during the time of slavery. People sang them to express the grief and suffering to which they were often subject. The music soothed their own souls and those of their listeners. It presented religious, usually Christian, sentiments in a distinctly African style. From the United States of America to Europe and to the rest of the world, Negro spirituals have made a special mark on world music.

The Visual Arts

From their earliest beginnings, the people of Africa have expressed themselves through the visual arts. Rock paintings of very ancient times have been discovered in many parts of Africa.

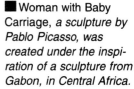 ■ Woman with Baby Carriage, *a sculpture by Pablo Picasso, was created under the inspiration of a sculpture from Gabon, in Central Africa.*

Stone and wood carvings abound in African villages and homes. True works of art, they have found a place in museums and in the homes of American and European collectors as well. Originally all of these objects had a religious purpose.

African religion is a religion without scripture and originally without written records. At one time, people therefore concluded that it was a religion of illiteracy and without record. But in fact, records of African religion are many. Some of the most important of these are its visual arts.

African visual arts have influenced some of the great Western artists of the 20th century. Among these were Pablo Picasso and Henri Matisse. Matisse recalled how an African statuette, with its strong character and purity of line, influenced Picasso's style and led to the birth of *cubism,* one of the most important movements of modern art. Picasso well understood the connection between African art and religion. He wrote, "My greatest artistic revelation came about when I was suddenly struck by the sublime beauty of the sculpture done by the anonymous artists of Africa. In their passionate and rigorous logic, these works of sacred art are the most powerful and beautiful products of the human imagination."

African Religion and Other Religions

African religion is a vital part of the African heritage, and Africans who live on the African continent belong to that heritage. They are culturally connected to African religion. However, not all African people today claim to be adherents of African religion. Many of them are declared Christians or Muslims.

In order to convert African people to Christianity or Islam, Christian and Muslim leaders have to understand the importance of African religion in African culture. The African people are African first and always. Their understanding of religion in general has been nurtured through African religion. An African, then, who becomes a Christian, becomes a Christian whose Christianity is grafted onto his or her Africanness. Today, leaders from other religions understand that they must first be able to talk meaningfully with others about the religion they have grown up in as well as the one they are adopting. Not long ago, the missionary effort was aimed at erasing African religion from the African continent and the world. Today, however, the message is one of dialogue. That this is happening is a further assurance that African religion will continue to prosper. Far from being wiped out by the influx of other religions, African religion continues to thrive.

African Religion as a Subject of Study

Only recently has African religion become a serious subject for study. Early students of African culture tended to see only what they wanted to see—exotic ritual and mysterious rites that meant nothing to them. They reported on its color and strangeness, but without understanding. Since that time, anthropologists, scientists who study humans, have conducted many studies of African religion that have promoted a better understanding. They have greatly contributed to assuring African religion a place among world religions.

During the late 1950s, along with African independence, Africans developed a keen awareness of their religion. They began to study it as never before. Books and textbooks appeared on the subject. In the United States, Harvard University inaugurated the teaching of African religion in 1977. Since that time, African religion has become a popular subject of study at colleges and universities, and at the high school level. The introduction of African religion into world educational systems is another sign that it is thriving.

African Religion as an Organization

African religion is usually called a "traditional religion," one that is spontaneously passed down from generation to generation. It has not been considered an "organized religion," in the sense that it does not have an elected church leader, a church hierarchy, and elected officials to run the business of the church and rule on matters of doctrine. However, African religion does have an internal structure. It is first of all a dynamic and living religion. Its leaders regard their religion as a whole consisting of interdependently coordinated parts. In recent years, leaders of African religion have begun to apply practices of organization and association to African religion. For that reason, today, in Africa and in other countries where African religion exists, it is becoming increasingly organized.

Other aspects of African religion are becoming increasingly organized as well. One of these is healing. Practically all African countries have taken initiatives to establish organizations and associations through which members of the healing communities may work together, for example by exchanging notes for the material and spiritual well-being of the people. Organizations such as the Uganda Herbalists and Cultural Association in Uganda and the Traditional Doctors' Association in South Africa are two of these.

The rest of the world is interested in African healing as well. International drug companies are working to understand the healing knowledge that the medicine men and women possess, particularly with regard to healing herbs. In the invaluable knowledge of the African healers may lie the treasure that sets off the new "scramble for Africa." Through their efforts, the knowledge and the secrets of the African healers will be preserved for the future.

Importantly for African religion, the knowledge and secrets of the healers cannot be cut away from their religious connections. It is ironic that only a few generations ago, the Western world seemed determined to stamp out African religion. Today, whether consciously or not, multinationals seem to be scrambling to promote its future.

The Future of African Religion

Colonial administrators in Africa called Africans "This incurably religious people." Are Africans really "incurably religious"? Certainly, most Africans seem to exhibit an inborn spirituality. African religion is deeply embedded in their being. Thus, as long as African people uphold their Africanness, respect their heritage, and update it to meet the circumstances of the changing world, African religion is assured of a future.

■ *The Magic of the Great Zimbabwe*

"The Great Zimbabwe" is the name given to ancient stone ruins in the country of Zimbabwe. These ruins, which include massive walls, a stone tower, an acropolis, or cluster of buildings on a hilltop, go back many hundreds of years and testify to Africa's ancient culture.

I think the place is well over a thousand years old. Somewhere some day we may argue the case. Here is where we redeem the half promise. Any book about the magic of Africa which did not include a word about the Great Zimbabwe, as it is called, would be unthinkable.

The first thing which strikes one is the large expanse of ruined stone dwellings, huddled together at a respectful distance from the great buildings of the temple and fort, reminding one irresistibly of the silent City of the Dead sprawling in its solitary decrepitude under the serene gaze of the Sphinx.

— *Witchcraft and Magic of Africa*, by Frederick Kaigh. London: Richard Lesley & Co. Ltd., 1947, pp. 91, 92.

GLOSSARY

Aksum or Axum—The name of a capital and of an ancient kingdom of Ethiopia.

Amharic—The official language of Ethiopia.

Ancestors—African forebears whose distinguished position in a community qualify their spirits to be regarded with veneration.

Associates of God—In an African religious setting these are the deities, the divinities, or the gods holding spiritual power that is subordinated to the power of the Supreme Being.

Candomblé—A Brazilian version of Yoruba religion.

Chwuku—The name by which the Igbo people of Nigeria call God. It means the "Great Spirit."

Copts—Indigenous Egyptians.

Cubism—A style of painting and sculpture noted for the reduction of natural forms to geometric ones, which, to a certain extent, came to exist by the influence of African art.

Da—The Fon divinity of the cult of the serpent.

Divination—The art of interpreting human events and situations, discovering the past, revealing future events, and obtaining any required information by using specified techniques.

Diviner—A ritual leader who is qualified to conduct the art of divination.

Duality—A term applied to the African concept of God, in which God is understood to be One but in two constituents.

Ebasi—The name of God for the Duala people of Cameroon. It means "the Omnipotent Father."

Esu—The divinity in the Yoruba pantheon of gods who is charged with the office of inspector general in the theocratic government of God.

Ethnic group—A community or a people that share a common distinctive culture, religion, language, and other connecting links. In an African context the term is preferred as a substitute of the colonially loaded and misused word *tribe*.

Extrahuman forces—Mystical forces that include, magic, witchcraft, and sorcery.

Fa—The Fon divinity of divination.

Falasha—A member of the African Ethiopian Jewish community.

Fon—A people of Benin, formerly known as Dahomey, whose religion on the basis of its concept of Vodun has had a noticeable influence in the Western Hemisphere.

Ggulu—The divinity of the sky in the Baganda pantheon of gods.

Guardian spirit—A spirit identified as watching over the interests of a group of people, such as an extended family, a clan, or an ethnic group. Such spirits are symbolized by mountains, extraordinary trees, rocks, waterfalls, animals, reptiles, etc.

Healer—A ritual leader who is endowed with the knowledge of herbal medicine by superhuman powers, inheritance, and training. Interchangingly, he or she may be referred to as a medicine-man/woman, a herbalist, and many other familiar names in local languages such as mganga.

Herbalist—A person who conducts healing practices with superhuman assistance by use, mainly, of herbal medicine.

Heroes—Legendary personalities whose feats in a community have distinguished them sometimes to the extent of being made into gods.

Imana—The primary name used by the Banyarwanda and Barundi of Central Africa to express their concept of God.

iNkosi yeZulu—The Lord of the sky or heaven.

Jakuta—The divinity and functionary of God's ministry of justice in the Yoruba pantheon of gods.

Kaffir—A person who has no faith; an infidel, unbeliever.

Kaffirism—A system of unbelief.

Kaffraria—A land of unbelievers.

Katonda—The name the Baganda of Uganda use to call God. It means "Creator," "Originator."

Kazooba—The name for God used by some African peoples, such as the Bazinza of Tanzania, Banyankore, and the Baganda of Uganda. The name means "the Sun," which is here metaphorically used to mean the Supreme Being.

Kibuuka—The divinity of war in the Baganda pantheon of gods.

Kitaka—The earth divinity in the Baganda pantheon of gods.

Kiwanuka—The divinity of thunder, lightning, and fertility in the Baganda pantheon of gods.

Kwanzaa—The holiday based on the African first fruits celebrations intended to pay tribute to the rich cultural roots of African Americans.

Kwoth—The name used by the Nuer of Sudan to express their concept of God. It means "spirit."

Kyala—The name for God among the Nyakyusa of Tanzania. It means "Owner of all things."

Legba—The divine trickster in the Fon religion. Legba determines the fortunes and misfortunes of people; he is the messenger between God and other gods.

Leve—The name for God among the Mende in Sierra Leone. It means "the High Up One."

Leza—The name used by the Ambo and Baila of Zambia to express their concept of God. It means "Creator."

Lubaale—The pantheon of the Baganda religion of Uganda. Katonda, the Baganda name for the Supreme Being, is not strictly part of *lubaale*. He is above *lubaale* as the Creator and metaphorical father of the Balubaale, the plural form of *lubaale*.

Mabee—The name by which the Bulu people of Cameroon call God. It means "The One who bears the world."

Macumba—A Brazilian version of the Yoruba religion.

Magic—The ability and practice of manipulating mysterious forces for practical ends.

Mangu—An innate substance in a person's body that is believed to carry the germ of witchcraft.

Mawu-Lisa—The hyphenated divinity that makes up the Fon pantheon of the sky gods. Mawu is female and Lisa is male; together they advance the work of creation initiated by Nana-Buluku.

Medium—A person endowed with the capability of being possessed by a spirit.

Mhondoro—Spirits that were associated with the ruling dynasties of Great Zimbabwe.

Modimo—The name for God among the Tswana people of Southern Africa. It means "Greatest Ancestral Spirit."

Monotheism—A system of a belief in One God.

Mukasa—The divinity of fertility, health, wealth, and general welfare in the Baganda pantheon of gods.

Mulungu—The name for God among the Gogo ethnic group of Tanzania and the Chewa ethnic group of Malawi.

Musisi—The divinity in charge of earthquakes in the Baganda pantheon of gods.

Musoke—The rainbow spirit in the Baganda pantheon of gods.

Mvelamqandi—The name for God among the Swazi people of Swaziland. It means "The One who appears first."

Mwari—The name of the Supreme Being as believed by the Shona people of Zimbabwe.

Nana-Buluku—The name used by the Fon people of Benin, formerly known as Dahomey, to express the idea of the Supreme Being as the Creator.

Ngai—The name for God used by the Gikuyu and Akamba ethnic groups of Kenya. It is also used by the Masai, who live both in Kenya and Tanzania. The name means "The Creator, the Divider, the Benefactor, the Possessor of Brightness."

Nyambi—The name for God as the Supreme Being and Creator of everything, as believed by the Barotse people of Zambia. Their concept of God is particularized by their belief that Nyambi had a wife whose name is Nasilele.

Nyame—The name for God among the Ashanti of Ghana. It means "Shining One."

Nzambi—The name by which the Vili people of the Congo know God. It means "Creator and Ultimate Source of Power."

Ogun—The divinity of war and iron in the Yoruba pantheon of gods; patron of all works connected with iron, and presiding divinity over matters concerned with oaths, covenants, and pacts.

Olodumare—The name for God among the Yoruba people. It means "Most Supreme Being."

Onyankopon—The name for God among the Akan people of Côte d'Ivoire and Ghana. It means "Alone the Great One."

Orisa—The pantheon of the Yoruba religion.

Orisanla—The archdivinity of the Yoruba pantheon of gods. This divinity is also known as Obatala, who in the theocratic arrangement of Yoruba religion holds the position of associate creator.

Orunmilla—The divinity of divination and prognostics in the Yoruba pantheon of gods.

Pantheon—In African religious context, all national gods collectively considered.

Phansi—The habitation place of spirits, which is believed by the Zulu to be below the surface of the earth.

Polytheism—The system of belief in hierarchically graduated and many gods.

Priest—The overseer, administrator, and coordinator of matters that relate to divine premises, such as a temple of a god. The priest officiates over the rites pertaining to the temple and sacred grounds.

Quarternity—The African conceptualization of God as One but in four constituents.

Rainmaker—A person endowed with the capability of effectively praying for the rain to fall and praying for it to stop.

Rites—Ceremonial, customary, and prescribed practices that punctuate all aspects of life in African religion.

Rites of Passage—In African religion, the ceremonies, customs, and practices that are performed in order to religiously enable people, from their earliest to their latest moment of existence on earth, to move smoothly through turning points of one's life.

Ritual—The actualization of a belief system.

Rog—The name for God among the Serer of Gambia and Senegal. It means "Creator."

Ruhanga—The name by which the Banyankore and Banyoro of Uganda know the Supreme Being. It means "Creator and Fixer of everything."

Ruwa—The name by which the Chagga of Tanzania know God. It means "The Sun."

Sagbata—The Fon divinity of the earth.

Sango—Like Jakuta, a Yoruba divinity and functionary in God's ministry of justice.

Se—The Fon divinity of the souls of human beings.

Sogbo—The Fon divinity of thunder and the sea.

Sorcery—Wicked magic intended to hurt others.

Spirit—A bodiless and superhuman power, force, or vital element, which human beings are mindful of with reverence.

Spirit World—Spirits collectively considered.

Spirits of the Departed—The souls of particular human beings and other animated creatures, which at the point of separation from the body are transformed into spirits, and are regarded with reverence.

Spiritual guardian—A spirit identified as watching over the interests of a group of people.

Suku—The name for God among the Ovimbundu of Angola. It means "He who supplies the needs of His creatures."

Superhuman beings—Gods, ancestors, guardian spirits, and spirits of the departed, who are regarded as powers above human beings.

Supreme Being—God as the unique power above which is no other.

Taboo—A prohibition from doing something or using something because of its reverential nature.

Ubuntu—Being truly human.

Uluhlanga—The name for God used by the Ngoni people of Malawi. It means "The Original Source."

Unity—A term applied to the ideas of the Supreme Being and the concept of God to reflect God being One and uniquely one.

Unkulunkulu—The name for God used by the Zulu of South Africa and the Ndebele of Zimbabwe. It means "The Great Oldest One."

Vidye—The name by which the Baluba of Congo know the Supreme Being. It means "Great Creator Spirit."

Vital force—The invisible power that is believed to underlie and energize a variety of objects of God's creation.

Vodun—The Fon pantheon of gods.

Walumbe—The divinity of death in the Baganda pantheon of gods.

Wanga—The divinity charged with fixing what goes wrong in the Baganda pantheon of gods.

Wene—The name for God among the Tallensi ethnic group of Burkina Faso. It means "Sky God."

Witch—A person who has in himself or herself an innate power or force of witchcraft.

Witchcraft—A cause of misfortune in a community.

Yala—The name for God among the Kpelle of Liberia.

Yataa—The name for God among the Kono people of Sierra Leone. It means "The One you meet everywhere."

Zambi—The name by which the Baya of the Central African Republic know God. It means "Creator."

Zulu—The sky or heaven.

CHAPTER NOTES

pages 23–24   J.F. Bierlein, *Parallel Myths*. New York: Ballantine Books, 1994, pp. 48–49

pages 25–26   Barbara Sproul, *Primal Myths: Creation Myths Around the World.* 1979, pp. 35–36

pages 28–29   John Roscoe, *The Baganda: An Account of Their Native Customs and Beliefs.* London: Macmillan & Co. Ltd., 1911

pages 29–31   Emmanuel V. Asihene, *Traditional Folk-Tales of Ghana.* Lewiston, New York: The Edwin Mellen Press, 1997

page 34   cf. Noel Q. King, *Religions of Africa.* New York: Harper & Row, Publishers, 1970

page 49–51   A.M. di Nola, ed., *The Prayers of Man.* London: William Heinemann, 1962

pages 98–101   cf. A.M. di Nola, ed., *The Prayers of Man.* London: Heinemann, 1962

page 101   cf. G. Lienhardt, *Divinity and Experience: The Religion of the Dinka.* Oxford: Clarendon Press, 1961

page 113   John Richardson, *A Life of Picasso.* New York: Random House, 1991, p. 488 n.24

FOR FURTHER READING

Brodd, Jeffrey. *World Religions: A Voyage of Discovery*. Winina, Minnesota: Christian Brothers Publications, 1997.

Idowu, E. Bolaji. *African Traditional Religion: A Definition*. London: SCM Press Ltd., 1973.

Kenyatta, Jomo. *Facing Mount Kenya*. London: Secker and Warburg, 1974.

King, Noel Q. *African Cosmos: An Introduction to Religion in Africa*. Belmont, California: Wadsworth Publishing Company, 1986.

Lawson, E. Thomas. *Religions of Africa: Traditions in Transformation*. San Francisco: Harper and Row Publishers, 1985.

Mbiti, John S. *Introduction to African Religion*. Suffolk: Heinemann, 1991.

———. *Prayers of African Religions*. London: SPCK, 1975.

Parrinder, Geoffrey. *West African Religion*. London: Epworth Press, 1978.

Shorter, Ayward. *Prayer in the Religious Traditions of Africa*. New York and Nairobi: Oxford University Press, 1976.

INDEX

!Kung Religion, 8

Abaluyia people of Kenya, sacrificial rites of passage, 72
Acholi religion, 8
Adinkira. *see* Ashanti
Africa, colonization, 17–18; continent, 10–11; history, 10, 14–18; independence, 106; origins of humanity, 11
African religion, acceptance as a world religion, 105–106; beliefs, 12–13; and Christianity, 108–109, 113; future of, 115; goals, 19; and Harvard University, 113–114; illness and healing, 11, 13; influence on worldwide religions, 107–109; music, 71, 109–111; organization, 114–115; origins and practices, 11; study of, 113–114; structure, 12; Ubuntu, 106–107, 121; unity and diversity, 19. *see also* Oral tradition
Akamba people of Kenya, Mumbi (name for God), 43; religion, 8
Akan people of Côte d'Ivoire, art, 34; Onyankopon (name for God), 44; proverbs, 32; Supreme Being and creation, 38
Akikuyu religion, 8
Aksum or Axum, 117
Aksumite religion. *see* Obsolete religions
Akuba. *see* Ashanti people
Alexander the Great, 15
Algiers, 9
Alur people of Uganda, Jok (name for God), 43
Amazi y'Imana rite. *see* Banyarwanda people
Ambo people of Zambia, Leza (name for God), 42, 119
Amharic, 117
Amulets, charms, 15
Ananse, Father Ananse, 26, 29–31
Ashanti people of Ghana, Adinkara designs, 9, 34; akuba figurine, 85; Asantehene (king), 80; Gye Nyame design, 9, 34; kontonkorowi stool, 77; Nyame (name for God), 44, 120; puberty prayer, 68; religion, 8; Nyankopon Tweaduapon Nyame, 68; Nyame symbol, 38;

Supreme Being as controller and sustainer of the universe, 39–40
Aspects of Bemba, The, 37
Associates of God. *see* Spirit world
Ateso religion, 8
Azande people of Sudan, and magic or ngwa, 94, 97; and witchcraft or mangu, 97, 119

Babalawo. *see* Yoruba people: Orunmila
Babemba religion, 8
Bachagga religion, 8
Bacongo people of Angola, Nzambi (name for God), 45; religion, 8
Bafipa religion, 8
Baganda people of Uganda, Ggulu, 55, 117; Katonda (name for God), 43, 119; Kibuuka, 58, 100, 118; Kitaka, 56, 118; Kiwanuka, 57, 118; Lubaale Mukasa, 27–29, 50; Lubaale Wannema, 28; Mukasa, 28, 50, 57–58, 119; Musisi, 56, 110, 119; Musoke, 119; Muwanga, 58; Nnambuubi, 28; Olubaale (dome of the sky), 55; pantheon of gods (Lubaale), 55–58, 118, 119; prayer, 58; religion, 8; rites of pregnancy, 65; Ssekabaka Muteesa II, King, 74; Sseerwanga, 28; Ssemagumba, 28; Supreme Being as possessor, 41; Supreme Being as provider, 41; Walumbe, 56, 122; Wanga, 56, 122
Bagisu religion, 8
Bahaya religion, 8
Bahehe religion, 8
Baila people of Zambia, Leza (names for God), 42, 119; Supreme Being and creation, 38
Baka religion, 8
Bakiga people, Supreme Being as provider, 41
Bakota people of the Republic of Congo, mbulu-ngulu or reliquary, 110
Balovedu people of South Africa, Queen, 80
Baluba people of Congo (Kinshasa), religion, 8; Vidye (name for God), 42, 121

Bamakonda religion, 8
Bambara people, Bemba or Ngala (Supreme Being), 37; Bemba, Nyale, Faro, or Ndomadyiri aspects of God, 37; religion, 8
Bambuti people of Congo, religion, 8; initiation, 66; Supreme Being as controller and sustainer of the universe, 40
Bamum people, Njinyi (name for God), 42
Bandembu religion, 8
Banyakyusa religion, 8
Banyamwezi religion, 8
Banyankore people of Uganda, Ruhanga (name for God), 43, 121; religion, 8; Supreme Being and creation, 38
Banyarwanda people of Rwanda, Central Africa, Amazi y'Imana rite, 64; Imana (name for God), 43, 64, 118; religion, 8; Supreme Being and creation, 38
Banyoro people, religion, 8; Ruhanga (name for God), 121
Barmum people of Cameroon, name for God, 42
Bartose people of Zambia, creation myth, 24–26; Kamonu, 25–26; Litoma, 26; Nasilele, 25, 120; Nyambi (name for God), 42, 120; Spider. *see* Ananse
Barundi people of Central Africa, Imana (name for God), 43, 118; religion, 8; Supreme Being as possessor, 41; and witchcraft, 97
Basonge people of Democratic Republic of Congo, mask, 57
Basukuma religion, 8
Basuto people of Lesotho, Molimo (name for God), 45
Baya people of Central African Republic, Zambi (name for God), 42, 122
Bazinza people of Tanzania, Kazooba (name for God), 43, 118
Bemba people of Central Africa, and magic, 94
Benin, and African religion, 9, 10; symbol of ritual power, 31
Berber religion. *see* Obsolete religions

Reverend Elder (Kikuyu word for God), 6

Rites of passage, aging, 69; birth and childhood, 62–63; death and funerals, 69–70; final funeral rites, 69–70; marriage, 68; naming rites, 65–66; pregnancy, 63–64; puberty and initiation, 67–68; taboos, 64, 121. *see also* Prayer

Rituals, 13, 15, 19, 49, 70, 87, 120; communal, 72–73; leadership, 73–75; objects, 90; sculpture, 90

Rog. *see* God, names for

Roman Empire. *see* Africa: history

Ruhanga. *see* God, names for

Ruwa. *see* God, names for

Sacred space, and animals, 83–84; and geography, 84; Great Zimbabwe, 83, 84, 89, 115; household, 90–91; natural world, 86–87; places and objects, 87; shrines, 88; sky, 84–86; temples, 87–88; tombs, 88; Uganda Museum, 82

Sacrifices, 13, 72, 87

Sagbata. *see* Fon people

Sahara and Sub-Sahara, 10–11

San religion, 8

Sango. *see* Yoruba people

Se. *see* Fon people: lesser gods

Senegal, Senegalese, 22, 99

Serer people of Gambia and Senegal, Rog (name for God), 44, 121

Shilluk people of Sudan, Juok (name for God), 43; religion, 8

Shinto, 11

Shona people of Zimbabwe, mhondoro, 88, 119; Mwari (name for God), 45, 84, 119; religion, 8; temple, 88. *see also* Sacred space: Great Zimbabwe

Slave trade, 17

Sogbo. *see* Fon people

Sorcery. *see* Mystical forces

Sotho religion, 8

Spirits, 13, 121

Spirit world, ancestors, 48, 117, 121; and African peoples, 61; associates of God, 46, 117; guardians, 13, 48–49, 118, 121; hierarchy of, 46–47, 51, 121; intermediaries, 48, 88; medium, 50, 119; superhuman beings, 19, 46, 49, 121

Spirits of the departed. *see* Spirit world

Spiritual guardians. *see* Spirit world

Ssekabaka Muteesa II. *see* Baganda people

Ssese Islands, 28

Storytellers, 20, 22

Suku. *see* God, names for

Superhuman beings. *see* Spirit world

Supreme Being, 19, 23, 26, 32, 33; attributes, 37–41, 121; controller and sustainer of universe, 39–40; creator of all things, 37, 38; and duality, 59, 117; God in one, two, or four, 36–37; and monotheism, 34–36, 119; and mountains, 40; hierarchy of gods, 36; and polytheism, 35–36, 41; and quarternity, 59, 120; unity, 59

Swazi people of Swaziland, Mvelamqandi (name for God), 45, 119; religion, 8

Taboo. *see* Rites of passage

Tallensi people of Burkina Faso, Wene (name for God), 44, 122

Tiv religion, 8

Taoism, 11

Togo, 9, 10

Tripoli, 9

Tswana people of Botswana, Modimo (name for God), 45, 119; religion, 8

Tunis, 9

Tutu, Archbishop Desmond Mpilo, 107

Ubuntu. *see* African religion

Uganda, East Africa, 38

Uluhlanga. *see* God, names for

Unity. *see* Supreme Being

Unkulunkulu. *see* God, names for

Vidye. *see* God, names for

Vili people of Congo (Brazzaville), Nzambi (name for God), 42, 120

Visual arts, cubism, 112, 117; and Henri Matisse, 112; and Pablo Picasso, 110, 111; rock paintings, 111–112

Vital force, 122

Vodun. *see* Fon people

Walumbe. *see* Baganda people

Wanga. *see* Baganda people

Wene. *see* God, names for

Witch doctors. *see* Mystical forces; Religious leadership

Witchcraft. *see* Mystical forces

Worship, 19, 70, 72

Xhosa religion, 8

Yala. *see* God, names for

Yataa. *see* God, names for

Yoruba people of Nigeria, creation myth, 22–24; Esu, 52–53, 117; Father of Mysteries (diviner), 77; Ifa, 52, 60; Ile Ife, 23, 87; iwa, 53; Jakuta and Sango, 4–55, 118; names for God, 44; Ogun, 53–55, 87, 88, 120; Olodumare or Olorun, 23–24, 44, 51, 52–53, 120; Orisha Nla, 23–24; Orisanla or Obalata, 52; Orunmilla, 52, 60, 77; pantheon of gods (Orisa), 52, 120; people, 6; religion, 8; shrine, 88; temple of Ife, 88

Zambi. *see* God, names for

Zulu people of South Africa, iNkosi yeZulu, 84, 118; phansi or sacred space, 84, 120; religion, 8; sky or heaven, 122; Supreme Being and creation, 38; Supreme Being as controller and sustainer of the universe, 40; Unkulunkulu (name for God), 45, 122; wedding rite, 71